Professor David Cesarani
13 November 1956–25 October 2015

The late **Professor David Cesarani**'s many publications included: The Making of Modern Anglo-Jewry (1990); Justice Delayed: How Britain Became a Refuge for Nazi War Criminals (1992); The Jewish Chronicle and Anglo-Jewry 1841–1991 (1994); Eichmann: His Life and Crimes (2004) which won the 2006 National Jewish Book Award for History in the USA; Major Farran's Hat: Murder, Scandal and Britain's War Against Jewish Terrorism, 1945–1948 (2008) and Final Solution: The Fate of the Jews 1933–1949 (2016, published posthumously).

He advised institutions, NGOs and government bodies on Holocaust and post-Holocaust and was a key figure in both the establishment of Holocaust Memorial Day and the Holocaust Exhibition at the Imperial War Museum. He was also adviser to the All Party Parliamentary War Crimes Group.

Professor Cesarani acted as historical consultant on numerous radio and TV documentaries including the Oscar-winning 'Into the Arms of Strangers: Stories of the Kindertransport' (2000); 'The Holocaust on Trial', BBC2 (2001); 'I Met Adolf Eichmann', BBC2 (February 2002); 'Auschwitz: The Forgotten Evidence', Channel 4 (December 2004) and 'Auschwitz: The Nazis and the Final Solution', BBC2 (January–February 2005).

In 2005, Professor Cesarani was awarded an OBE for services to Holocaust Education.

He died in October 2015.

*

Rt Hon Gordon Brown was Prime Minister of the United Kingdom of Britain and Northern Ireland and Leader of the Labour Party from 2007 to 2010. Prior to that he served as Chancellor of the Exchequer from May 1997.

*

Dawn Waterman is Heritage and Archive Adviser at the Board of Deputies of British Jews. Dawn and David were married until his untimely death in October 2015. They have two children, Daniel and Hannah.

The Left and the Jews | The Jews and the Left

David Cesarani

NO PASARAN MEDIA LTD
New Derwent House, 69–73 Theobalds Road,
London, England, WC1X 8TA
www.nopasaran.media

First published in Great Britain in 2004 by Labour Friends of Israel
This edition is published by No Pasaran Media Ltd in 2021

Acknowledgements for photographs:
Mark Gerson, 27 July 1998, National Portrait Gallery, London

A catalogue record of this book is available from the British Library

ISBN: Print: 978-1-9162357-4-8; Kindle: 978-1-9162357-5-5;
eBook: 978-1-9162357-6-2

2 3 4 5 6 7 8 9 NPM 25 24 23 22 21

Typeset in Minion by MacGuru Ltd

Published by: No Pasaran Media, an imprint of Dolman Scott Ltd
www.dolmanscott.co.uk

This republishing is done with the expressed permission of David Cesarani's widow Dawn Waterman and their two children, Daniel and Hannah. No Pasaran Media wants to add a special thanks to Dawn, Daniel and Hannah for their help, support and cooperation in the reprinting of this important piece of work.

To find our more about our authors and books, visit *www.nopasaran.media* and sign up for our newsletters

Contents

Foreword

by Rt Hon Gordon Brown

I worked with David Cesarani many years ago when I asked him to help me with a speech I was making on antisemitism. The notes he sent me for that speech turned into the pamphlet you are about to read. Over the many years since, I have had reason to be grateful for the advice he gave me then.

It is, as David rightly recognises, impossible to deny the closeness of, and the achievements brought about by, the strong links between the Jewish communities and the progressive Left. The litany of Jewish figures who provided both practical and intellectual contributions to every group on the socialist Left, and each Labour government here in the UK, is so extensive that marking some individuals out when I could mention so many is invidious.

David stands in this tradition, and were it not for him being taken from us far too soon, I know that he would have made an important direct contribution to the debate over the last few years.

As David writes, 'the Left has not always taken antisemitism seriously'. Indeed, it was as a result of my concern about the rise of the 'new antisemitism' in Britain and Europe that, while serving as Chancellor of the Exchequer in 2002, I asked David to write the aforementioned paper.

David's warning to all of us then – that 'there are signs that in treating Jewish fears about anti-Jewish sentiment as merely a device to muzzle criticism of Israel ... [the Left] is in danger of repeating the historic error of those ... who dismissed hatred of Jews and threats to their well-being as merely a delusion and the symptom of an ephemeral conflict' – should have been heeded by the Labour Party itself. Had it been, this would have headed off the morally and politically catastrophic growth of antisemitism within the Left.

I am proud of Labour's record in government between 1997 and 2010 in tackling antisemitism. We invested in the security of Jewish schools, reformed how race and religious hate crimes were prosecuted, and provided funding to the Holocaust Educational Trust to ensure young people understood its truth and contemporary relevance.

The Holocaust Educational Trust is now an essential part of our society and I remember well the influence it has had on young people who, in my own constituency, came back from a school visit to Auschwitz determined to warn the whole town of the evil that antisemitism can do. In our memorial gardens is a plaque from their Anne Frank Week with wise words from the late Jonathan Sacks inscribed on it.

Having spoken at the planning enquiry in support of its construction, I hope they will soon complement their work with the building of the UK Holocaust Memorial and Learning Centre.

Our record was part of a rich Labour tradition which is

brought to life in this work and I am proud of all those who continue to stand in, and fight for, that tradition.

In September 2018, I spoke at the Jewish Labour Movement's conference. I wanted to show the Jewish community that there were those of us in the Labour Party who were determined to make a stand and try to right the wrongs then being inflicted on the Jewish community. The fight we were engaged in was, I said, one for the very 'soul of the Labour Party'. The battle against racism is 'about who we are. Our conscience means we don't just stand up for the rights of some people, some of the time, it means we stand up for the rights of all who are oppressed, all of the time.'

If in recent years Labour failed to build resilience against antisemitism in our politics, we must correct this now under Keir Starmer's strong leadership.

As we seek to put the dark chapter of the last five years behind us, we must redouble our effort to rebuild Labour's relationship with the Jewish community. There will understandably be a great deal of suspicion on the part of British Jews and their communal organisations. We now have to acknowledge, and work to overcome, the deep and justified anger and hurt felt.

The next chapter of the story David so generously started for us is yet to be written. But I have confidence that with perseverance and a determination to stand up for what is right, we will overcome.

A preface
by Dawn Waterman

A public historian, David wrote for many different audiences in his career – fellow academics, students, newspaper and magazine readers, non-fiction readers, specialist and general audiences. But he only wrote one piece – the one on which this book is based – especially for the Chancellor of the Exchequer.

I'm told that – in between important meetings on funding public services and reducing child poverty in 2002 – Gordon Brown, then the Chancellor, was drawn into a conversation about antisemitism, in the UK and on the British Left.

In January, the *New Statesman* – the favourite journal of the Left in the UK – had appeared with a cover design depicting a golden star of David piercing a Union Jack flag and the headline 'a kosher conspiracy'. This was no isolated incident; six months previously, the late Tam Dalyell MP had told *Vanity Fair* that Prime Minister Tony Blair was 'unduly influenced by a cabal of Jewish advisers'. David had commented, trenchantly, on both.

This discussion, apparently, led to the Chancellor's wanting to know more. I remember very clearly when David put down the phone after speaking to Brown's advisor one Thursday evening:

'Gordon Brown wants a briefing on antisemitism on the Left' he reported. 'He needs it by Monday. I think we'll have to alter our plans for the weekend'.

David met the deadline and *The Left and the Jews, The Jews and the Left*, later published by Labour Friends of Israel, is the result.

Fast forward, a decade or so, and I am giving the hesped (Hebrew for eulogy) at David's stone-setting in July 2016. On that sunny afternoon at the cemetery, I reflected on the time since David had died:

'A favourite tweet came earlier this year at the height of the row about antisemitism in the Labour Party. You'll remember the uproar when Ken Livingstone said that Hitler "was a Zionist". The tweet read "Where is David Cesarani when you most need him?"'

Of course, I wasn't right that the Livingstone episode was the height of the row about antisemitism in the Labour Party. Not by a long chalk. But the sentiment expressed by the journalist (who had been at Cambridge at the same time as David) on Twitter was spot-on. I have often thought since what a shame it is that, at the moment it was most needed, David wasn't there to help us better understand and challenge the growth of antisemitism in the Labour Party.

We do, however, have *The Left and the Jews, The Jews and the Left* and my thanks are to No Pasaran Media for republishing it now.

1 Introduction

The relationship between Jews and the Left stretches back 150 years. Understanding it is important both for the history of the Jews and the history of socialism. The course of this complex, fascinating and often troubled relationship touches on central questions of Jewish existence and socialist thought. Despite the transformation of the political constellation since 1989, these questions remain as urgent as ever.

Historians, mostly Jewish, have routinely treated the subject in apologetic or pejorative terms, and not without good reason. The writing of modern Jewish history commenced in the shadow of anti-Jewish movements that routinely identified Jews with Marxism and widely feared revolutionary movements. Institutionalised anti-clericalism and the repression of most Jewish political life in the Soviet Union overshadowed an objective evaluation of the role played by Jews in the Russian Revolution. Jewish historians writing in the wake of the Nazi genocide against Europe's Jews, a catastrophe that the Left failed to stop and that seemed to expose the hollowness of slogans about fraternity, also saw socialism in a less than positive light. Consequently, many Jewish scholars tended to denigrate the ties between Jews and the Left, treating Jewish socialists as apostates or deluded idiots. They read forward from Marx, who was at best negative towards Jews in theory, or backwards from Stalin, who was at worst hostile in practice, and concluded that socialism from its theoretical inception to its most concrete embodiment held nothing but ill for Jewish people.[1]

It is certainly easy to assemble appalling anti-Jewish quotations emanating from the mouths or pens of leading socialist thinkers and activists from the middle of the nineteenth century to the present. But crude polemics of this kind rely on wresting statements out of their immediate context and ignore the bigger picture of relations between Jews and non-Jews. The Jewish–Left dyad is only one feature of a dynamic relationship stretching over centuries. It is marked both by the ravages of religious conflict and by the attempt to escape religiously determined attitudes. The troubled saga of Jewish–Christian relations clearly left its imprint on Christian Socialist attitudes towards the Jews, but attempts by socialists to transcend religion did not remove sources of ambivalence or even hostility towards Jewish particularity. Furthermore, despite the universalism of socialist principles, the interaction of Jews with the Left was always geographically and culturally specific. And it changed in nature over time as its social components altered. The relations between working class Polish Jews and Russian Bolsheviks in 1918 cannot be simply compared to the links between Black American New Leftists and middle class Jewish socialists in New York in the 1960s.[2]

This essay will survey the crucial ideas, movements, personalities, and turning points that characterised relations between Jews and the Left. It will treat the relationship as mutually dynamic, characterised by ambivalence on both sides. It begins with the Enlightenment and the ambiguity of rationalism when confronted by traditional religions and what we would today call ethnic groups. As far as the Jews were concerned, this ambivalence was first given tangible expression during the French Revolution. The emancipatory forces unleashed in 1789 eventually enabled Jews to participate fully in the mainstream of European social, economic and political life. However, the sudden prominence of a few Jews who benefited from economic liberalisation provoked a backlash from the Left. At roughly the same time, philosophical currents in Germany that embodied a critique of Judaism helped inspire scientific socialism. As a result, Marxism was both emancipatory and shot through with ambivalence towards the existence of the Jews as a separate faith group.

Marxism supplied the theoretical underpinning for a century of socialist activity. This essay will touch on the relations between Jews and the social democratic and labour movements in Western Europe and the USA, including relations with the emerging Jewish labour movement. It will examine the role of Jews in the Russian revolutionary parties and the situation of Jews in the early years of the USSR. Marxism also provided the framework for the Left to analyse the emergence of Jewish nationalism in the form of Zionism and the diaspora nationalism of the Bund – the Jewish socialist labour party of Russia and Poland. But mutual perceptions did not depend on ideology alone. They were dramatically affected by the rise of anti-semitic and anti-socialist parties in the 1880s, and by the impact of fascism after the First World War. This essay will look at the 'pink generation' between the two world wars when Jewishness and leftism were virtually congruent. After 1945, it was common to discuss the decline of Jewish socialism and to ascribe this to the ascent of a New Left that co-mingled anti-colonialism and anti-Americanism with anti-Zionism.

The essay will end with a discussion of how Jews and the Left have interacted since the 1980s. This conclusion will illustrate the strength of continuities between Enlightenment attitudes and contemporary positions, but also highlight unprecedented developments. These include the effect of 'Holocaust consciousness', the collapse of the Soviet bloc, the burgeoning of 'identity politics', and multiculturalism.

It is impossible to discuss Jews or the Left without adding a word about definitions. 'The Left' is a term that encompasses an historical constellation in constant flux. Socialism was born out of the Enlightenment. Indeed, it is arguable that its economic theory owes everything to just the Scottish Enlightenment. Theories of freedom, equality, and fraternalism were given practical shape during the French Revolution, although socialist movements and parties do not appear in a recognisable, modern form until the 1820s and 1830s. Marx and Engels then introduced a sharp distinction between 'scientific socialism' and all that preceded it. In the mid nineteenth century they and their followers forged the modern social democratic movements by marrying Marxist theory with revolutionary practice. Meanwhile, sundry anarchists and syndicalists developed and maintained an alternative vision of socialism. The Russian Revolution made the scene still more complicated. After 1918 the Socialist International represented Marxist and neo- and non-Marxist parties not aligned with Moscow, while the Bolsheviks established the Communist International as a rallying point for Marxist orthodoxy (and a tool of Soviet foreign policy). In the 1930s, Leon Trotsky set up the Third International in opposition to 'actually existing socialism'. After 1945, Maoism and the New Left added to the fractured landscape of the Left. Since the collapse of the Soviet Union the scene has mercifully simplified.[3]

While there was much in common ideologically between all segments of 'the Left', policy towards the Jews and 'Jewish issues' varied greatly. So, as far as possible, in this paper the section of the Left under discussion will be specified, although sweeping generalisations are unavoidable.

The definition of Jews and the Jewish Left is no less challenging. But as it is less familiar, the changing nature of Jewish identity – from traditional to secular by degrees – and shifting Jewish political allegiances will be spelled out as necessary. It has been suggested that there is an affinity between Jews and socialism on account of the story of the Exodus and the prophetic writings in the Hebrew Bible. This is debatable. What is more certain is that living as a diasporic minority for most of their history, Jews constituted small, enclosed communities that functioned as 'mini-welfare states' undergirded by traditions of *tzedakkah* or charity for the poor and needy. It is also evident that the experience of minority status fostered a strong preference for tolerant, pluralistic, rights-based polities. However, modern Jewish history suggests that individual Jews and entire communities became involved with socialism only after a rupture with the past. This paper uses fracture as the operating principle to explain how and why Jews came to intersect with the Left and how the Left contributed to that uncoupling from community and tradition.[4]

2 Enlightenment and revolution: the sources of inspiration and ambivalence

The European Enlightenment, personified by Jean-Jacques Rousseau and Voltaire, is well known as a source of emancipatory thought and revolutionary movements. Less well known is the Jewish Enlightenment, the *haskalah*, which followed in its wake, but which was the source of similar ferment within the Jewish world. Jewish revolutionaries were children of the *haskalah* in much the same way that the Jacobins owed their inspiration to the *philosophes*.

In 1750 the Jews of Europe lived a life apart from the majority population of the countries and domains in which they resided. Jews were a despised, alien minority. They lived under special Jewry laws that governed their choice of livelihood, place of residence, and even right to marry. Forbidden the right to own land or to trade and manufacture within Christian guilds of craftsmen and merchants, they were pushed to the margins of the economy or squeezed into its interstices. A small number enjoyed shaky prosperity as moneylenders, merchants, cattle or grain dealers; more were craftsmen and hand workers, mainly serving their own communities; most were poor, eking out a living as petty traders, market stall holders, pedlars, old-clothes men, and second-hand dealers. The typical image of 'the Jew' in paintings and prints of this era depicts a dirty, uncouth and foreign-looking character whose beard and side curls mark him out as ignorant and superstitious. Most of Jewish life was passed in autonomous communities, according to Jewish law, under the immediate supervision of rabbis and communal notables. In a number of communities throughout central Europe a few privileged Jews enjoyed greater freedom and the opportunity to share the lifestyle of gentiles. The members of this elite were the *hofjuden*, or court Jews. Their temporary privileges were held in return for providing local rulers with financial or other services. Another type of exception was to be found in port cities such as Bordeaux, Amsterdam, London and Trieste. In these maritime trading centres the dominant pragmatic mercantilist outlook allowed for the growth of cosmopolitan populations attracted by the promise of economic opportunity and religious toleration. Jewish refugees from the Inquisition had settled in these ports since the 1590s and flourished there.[5]

Mercantilism and toleration were two aspects of a broader change in attitudes towards Jewish people. Throughout Europe, absolutist rulers wanted to remove the structures that preserved the autonomy of social groups, be they churchmen, nobles, burgers or Jews, and maximise their direct fiscal contribution to the state. Thinkers were increasingly critical of discriminatory laws that violated the natural rights of men, particularly religious minorities, even if they happened to be Jews. Rationalists attacked practices that appeared to be validated only by the longevity of the prejudices they embodied. The *philosophes* were not freed of such prejudices, least of all when it came to Jews, but they were convinced that Jewish populations could shed what were commonly considered to be their objectionable features if the conditions under which they existed were improved. Given favourable circumstances, they might even shed their superstitious ways, embrace reason, and stop being Jews.[6]

Voltaire and Gotthold Ephraim Lessing represent two strands of Enlightenment thinking about the Jews that were to influence progressive thinkers, social reformers and politicians of the Left for a hundred years.

Voltaire excoriated received wisdom, superstition, myth and anything, including privilege, not founded on demonstrable reason or validated by observed experimentation. He persistently attacked the Old Testament because it contained the foundational myths of both Judaism and, more importantly, Christianity. To Voltaire, Christianity was one of the sources of social and political infamy, but the Church was powerful so he was careful to attack it obliquely. It was safer to lambast the creed from which Christianity had sprung and to which it was indissolubly linked. Thus Voltaire's statements about Jews were full of malice. In his *Dictionnaire Philosophique* (1764), he wrote: 'It is with regret that I discuss the Jews: this nation is, in many respects, the most detestable ever to have sullied the earth.' However, Voltaire advanced arguments for toleration and condemned religious discrimination against Jews. His animosity towards them was philosophical, not personal. To him, Judaism fostered the mythological basis of the belief systems he sought to destroy and suggested the possibility that a people whose existence was founded on wrong thinking could survive through the ages. Jewish resilience defied his prescription, and that of other *philosophes,* for changing and improving the world. Reason dictated that the Jews should disappear along with superstition and all religion. However, on the one hand they seemed impervious to reason while, on the other, they could not be extirpated. Voltaire's rage against the anomalous persistence of the Jews would be echoed by rationalist, materialist and progressive thinkers of the Left for generations to come.[7]

Voltaire played a key role in the modernisation and transmission of anti-Jewish discourse. Of course, Judaism had been a target of Christian polemic since the days of the Church fathers. Jews were stigmatised as Christ-killers who, in the person of Judas, rejected the true messiah, conspired against him and betrayed him for money. This was the basis for stereotyping Jews as stubborn, avaricious, treacherous and hostile to Christians. Over the centuries various additions and modifications were made to the litany of anti-Judaism, but these charges remained at the core. Through texts, iconography and preaching they were inscribed in popular culture and inculcated into the hearts and minds of churchgoers. However, while secularisation led to the deletion from popular belief of many other superstitions and irrational practices, anti-Jewish prejudice continued. It was Voltaire's achievement to secularise this prejudice, casting it as a rational response to Jewish behaviour in the past (as allegedly recorded in the Bible) and in the present.

It was in the nature of Jews, he maintained, to be money-loving and shifty. Their nature, more than their religion, was at fault. Racial thinking was to arrive on the scene decades after Voltaire's death, but by uncoupling anti-Jewish discourse from religion and anchoring it in ethnography he laid the foundations for racial theorists like Count Joseph Gobineau, Paul Lagarde and Houston Stewart Chamberlain. Voltaire also enabled the notion of Jews as financially adept, conspiratorial and fundamentally alien to coexist with the emancipatory impulses of the Enlightenment and every progressive ideology that descended from it. Thanks to him it became mandatory for progressives to contest religiously inspired anti-Jewish discrimination while at the same time aspiring to the transformation, even the evaporation, of the Jews.[8]

By contrast, Lessing accepted Jews for what they were and pleaded for their social inclusion. In his 1749 play *The Jews* and his 1779 drama *Nathan the Wise*, he challenged every negative stereotype of the Jews then current. If Jews were superstitious and followed despicable trades it was because they were denied schooling and the choice of a calling. The Jewish character in his 1749 play says: 'If two nations are to live together faithfully and uprightly, each must contribute an equal share. But what if one of them considers it a matter of religion, and practically a work of merit, to persecute the other?' Lessing befriended the self-educated Jewish philosopher Moses Mendelssohn who in his lifetime travelled from a traditional Jewish background to become one of the leading secular thinkers of his day. To Lessing, Mendelssohn proved that Jews were capable of reason and intellectual perfection, if given the chance to progress. While some intellectuals tried to convince Mendelssohn to convert, on the grounds that if he could master philosophy he must see the falseness of Judaism, Lessing defended his right to be a Jew and a philosopher.[9]

Mendelssohn was not just a master of European philosophy: he was a talmudic scholar and rabbi. As such he advocated a policy of enlightenment within Judaism, sought to revivify Hebrew, and tried to show that Biblical texts offered contemporary ethical guidance. He urged Jews to embrace secular education, diversify their professions and integrate: 'To be a Jew at home and a gentile on the street.' Mendelssohn condemned all forms of religious coercion and challenged the power of the rabbinate. He maintained that Judaism was a religion of reason that depended on voluntary adherence and, consequently, deserved equal status with other 'natural', i.e. reasonable, religions such as Christianity. Mendelssohn was thereby seeking to defend and rehabilitate traditional Judaism using modern philosophy, to make it attractive for young Jews, the scions of the *hofjuden*, who were exposed to secular learning and Enlightenment thought. But to some Christians he seemed to herald the dissolution of Judaism and an end to Jewish apartness. His Jewish followers and gentile admirers assumed that his reform agenda was keyed to achieving the end of Jewish exclusion and it was here that a religious programme collided with a social and political one, with revolutionary results.[10]

Mendelssohn was friendly with the educational and political reformer Christian Wilhelm von Dohm. When Mendelssohn was asked by the Jews of Alsace to intercede on their behalf against discriminatory and repressive laws he asked

Dohm to act on their behalf. Dohm obliged with a treatise entitled *On the Civil Improvement of the Jews* (1781), in which he argued that the exclusion of the Jews retarded general economic progress. He maintained that the Jews should be integrated into society and the state even though they had many disreputable features. They were petty, superstitious and morally corrupt – but that was only to be expected if they were treated like pariahs. They would only have an incentive to change and feel affection for their country and its people if they were put on an equal footing with other citizens. Dohm both articulated and reinforced a common perception of advanced thinkers on the eve of the French Revolution that the Jews were, indeed, inferior, but could be changed for the better. In this context, change entailed ceasing to live according to Jewish tradition and religious prescription.[11]

The French Revolution and the Declaration of the Rights of Man and the Citizen propelled the ideas of men like Dohm into the realm of policy-making. The announcement that all men were equal provoked the Jews of Bordeaux, who resided in the city thanks only to revocable privileges, to ask the National Assembly if that meant they were also now French citizens with all the rights that citizenship connoted. The petitioners were Sephardim: Jews of Spanish and Portuguese origin who had lived double lives as secret Jews or New Christians until they fled the Iberian peninsular. They were mostly prosperous merchants, urbane and fully acculturated. Yet their plea still posed a dilemma for the men of the Third Estate imbued with the ideas of Voltaire and Dohm. During the winter of 1789–90, the National Assembly debated at enormous length whether a Jew could be a citizen. It finally resolved that the Spanish and Portuguese Jews living in France could become citizens, but the Jews of Alsace, four times their number, were excluded. The Alsatian Jews were Ashkenazi, Yiddish speaking and Orthodox. They had lived for centuries under Jewry laws in small towns and villages where they made a living as pedlars, cattle and grain dealers, and money-lenders. Their emancipation would have to wait nearly two years until the progressive radicalisation of the revolution made such a daring act conceivable.[12]

The debates in the National Assembly during the winter of 1789–90 and the Constituent Assembly in 1791 set a pattern for progressive and Leftist politicians confronted by Jewish demands for equal treatment. During one of the exchanges, Count Stanislaus de Clermont-Tonnerre pronounced that: 'To the Jews as a nation everything is to be denied; everything should be given to them as individuals; they must not constitute a political body nor an order within the state; they must be citizens individually.' He added that Jewish communities which insisted on preserving their autonomy should be liquidated. Clermont-Tonnerre had observed that the Spanish and Portuguese Jews constituted a self-contained community, dubbed 'the *Naçion*', governed by Jewish law. He demanded that they disband their communal structure, surrender their peculiar identity, and live according to French law as French men and women. The Sephardim were only too happy to oblige, although they quietly reconstituted their communal institutions in another guise. The Alsatian Jews proved more resistant to such demands and only grudgingly gave up their communal autonomy. Even so, the revolutionary cadres were not content with these sweeping changes to Jewish life. Jews in Alsace were subjected to forced acculturation and integration aggravated by swelling anticlericalism. At the height of the Jacobin ascendancy, in addition to taking on all the duties of citizenship such as army service, Jews were compelled to close their places of worship, work on the Sabbath and rest only on the tenth day. Circumcision and the slaughter of cattle according to Jewish religious law were prohibited until the fall of the Jacobins.[13]

In a sense none of this was the result of anti-Jewish sentiment. It was the outcome of doctrinaire radical thinking and extreme rationalism. While Jews in France embraced the revolution because it offered them civic equality and social inclusion, they discovered that the very universalist principles that entitled them to emancipation were also at best insensitive or at worst inimical to Jewish particularity. This was to be, in a nutshell, the perpetual dilemma which the Left posed to the Jews when it championed emancipation with one hand while menacing the preservation of Jewish particularism with the other.

However, not all Jews saw the exchange of Jewish tradition for civil rights as a poor bargain. Some of the more radical acolytes of Moses Mendelssohn were propelled by the logic of Jewish enlightenment into a far-reaching critique of Judaism and Jewish difference. This led them to question the value of the traditions, practices and beliefs that separated Jews from Christians and that were used by Christian antagonists to justify the second class status of Jews. The willingness to trim Judaism and overthrow traditional authority was increased by their experience of revolution and reaction between 1800 and 1815. When the French revolutionary armies conquered countries and brought them under French influence, the ghetto walls were literally torn down and local Jews were granted the same equality that Jews enjoyed in France. But with the defeat of Napoleon and the restoration of the *ancien régime* these rights were revoked, often violently. Many young Jews who tasted freedom could not adjust to the revocation of emancipation. The parents of Karl Marx, for instance, converted and had him baptised so that his life and career would not suffer because he was a Jew. The poet Ludwig Börne converted in order not to lose his position as a public official. Börne went on to provide poetic inspiration for German socialists, but his radicalism stemmed in a large measure from his exposure to the radical critique of Judaism and traditional authority. He later wrote: 'As I was born a slave, I love freedom better than you. As I grew up a slave, I understand freedom more than you. As I had no fatherland to call my own, I long for it more passionately than you.'[14]

Other German Jews sought to remould Judaism to make it congruent with perceived Christian expectations and so win back emancipation. A group of young intellectual modernisers formed an association for the scientific study of Judaism – the *Verein für Kultur und Wissenschaft des Judentums* – to research Jewish texts to prove that Judaism could be adapted to contemporary mores. Their number included another future radical poet, Heinrich Heine. After attempting unsuccessfully to reconcile his Jewish identity with his environment through this form of scientific study, Heine converted. It was a searing experience. Like Börne, his anti-authoritarian stance, irreverence and penchant for critique bears the stamp of a uniquely Jewish dilemma. The first generation of socialist Jews was thrown up by the internal dynamic of Jewish thought as much as by circumstances. Their willingness to identify with oppressed and marginal groups was a reflection of their own odyssey, but they were first unhinged from Jewish tradition by the reform movement within Judaism itself.[15]

3 Socialism and the Jews from Saint Simon to Karl Marx

The emancipation of the Jews in France released a flood of energy and enterprise. Within thirty years Jews had migrated from the country to the towns, from the eastern provinces to Paris, and entered a new range of trades and professions. A tiny few, like the Rothschilds, achieved fabulous wealth. Yet to the early French socialists like Charles Fourier (1772–1837), there seemed to be a connection between the 'rise of the Jews' and the explosion of capitalist enterprise. He railed against the 'hordes of Jews and vagabonds' that had arrived in Paris from Alsace and rued emancipation as premature: the Jews should have been morally reformed before they were allowed to fully enter society. Instead they had infected society with their vices of avarice and sharp dealing, the core of capitalism. 'The Jews, with their commercial morality, are they not the leprosy and perdition of the body politic?' he asked. 'In short, the Jews, politically, are a parasitical sect that tend to invade commerce at the expense of the nationals of the states in question without identifying themselves with the fate of any single fatherland.' Nothing about this anti-Jewish sentiment was intrinsic to socialism. Fourier's communitarian vision is comparable with Robert Owen's in England, but Owen did not evince any hostility to Jews. Nor did another pioneer of socialist thought, Henri de Saint Simon (1760–1825). On the contrary, Saint Simon's interest in harnessing technology and business organisation for the common good led to a strongly pro-Jewish stance because he admired the entrepreneurial skills of Jews in France.[16]

Nevertheless, the conflation of anti-Jewish attitudes and anti-capitalism seemed to lodge at the core of French socialist discourse. Much of the responsibility for popularising this bogus analysis lay with Alphonse Toussenel (1803–85). Toussenel's critique of capitalism was eccentric to say the least: he claimed that a new financial feudalism had arisen and a new feudal class was ruling the state in its own rapacious interests. But he dubbed the new rulers Jews and his best-selling book was titled *Les Juifs rois de l'epoque, histoire de la feodalité financière* [The Jews, kings of the epoque; history of financial feudalism]. Toussenel was followed by Pierre-Joseph Proudhon (1809–65), the utopian socialist and later syndicalist who coined the definition 'Property is theft'. Proudhon, like Toussenel, was influenced by Voltaire, but he conjoined the critique of Judaism with an attack on Jews as avatars of capitalism. He commended Voltaire's sarcastic suggestion that the Jews should be sent back to Jerusalem: 'The Jew is the enemy of humankind. The race must either be sent back to Asia or exterminated … By the sword, by amalgamation, or by expulsion the Jew must be made to disappear.' As George Lichtheim, the historian of socialism, lamented: 'Anti-semitism could and did become an element of the primitive system of ideas in which the anti-capitalist reaction of the 1830s and 1840s at first presented itself.' Even if the conjunction was momentary and rooted in an early stage of socialist thought, it was of terrible long-term significance: 'the anti-capitalism and anti-Jewish themes were intertwined, [and] it took considerable time before they could be disentangled.'[17]

Fourier, Toussenel, and Proudhon were later to become the targets of 'scientific socialism' and were ridiculed by Karl Marx (1818–83), its progenitor. Unfortunately, Marx's critique of unscientific utopian, communitarian and syndicalist socialism did not extend to a rejection of the anti-Jewish discourse that infused it. This was because, like his predecessors, he was influenced by Enlightenment perceptions of Jews and Judaism as archaic and redundant. And his critique was accentuated by his own desire as a convert and the target of anti-Jewish abuse to distance himself from the Jewish people.[18]

Although Marx reacted against Hegel and his followers, his thought is rooted in Hegelianism. For Hegel (1770–1831), monotheistic Judaism was an essential stepping stone to Christianity and, hence, human progress towards realising the spirit of reason. However, the Jews had achieved monotheism at the expense of creating for themselves an all-powerful, unforgiving deity and living in a realm of abstract metaphysics outside nature. 'The subsequent condition of the Jewish people', he wrote, 'which continues up to the mean, abject, wretched circumstances in which they still find themselves today is all simply the consequences and elaborations of their original fate. By this fate – an infinite power which they set over and against themselves and have never conquered – they have been maltreated and will be maltreated until they appease it by the spirit of beauty and so annul it by reconciliation.' While in the 1820s Hegel advocated Jewish emancipation, he never altered his view that Judaism had been superseded by Christianity and that it expressed a profound alienation of man from the world. By contrast, one of his leading followers, Bruno Bauer (1809–82), totally rejected Jewish emancipation on the grounds that Judaism was exclusionary. In an essay published in 1843, the title of which coined the term 'The Jewish Question', he argued that: 'The emancipation of the Jew in a thorough, successful and secure fashion is only possible if they will be emancipated not as Jews, that is, as beings who must remain forever alien to Christians, but if they will make themselves human beings who will not be separated from their fellow creatures through some barriers falsely deemed to be essential.' In any case, the Jews did not need formal emancipation, since through 'money power' they held enormous influence: 'the Jew who may be without rights in the smallest of German states determines the fate of Europe'. True emancipation would only come with revolution and the emancipation of society.[19]

Bauer's essay on the 'Jewish Question' provoked Marx to write a riposte that became the foundation text for socialists confronting Jewish issues. 'Zur Judenfrage', 1844, is distinguished by particularly vituperative language about Jews and Judaism. 'Money', Marx announced, 'is the zealous god of Israel, beside which no other god may stand.' 'The god of the Jews has become secularised and is now the god of the world. Exchange is the true god of the Jew.' But Marx was not attacking Jews per se or engaging in abuse for its own sake. Indeed, he defended the emancipation of the Jews and mocked Bauer's position. He scolded Bauer for seeing only the 'sabbath Jew' who demanded equality of religion while overlooking the 'everyday Jew' who was the Jew of commerce. Bauer had got it all wrong: the problem was not that Jews lacked emancipation, but that society lacked emancipation from the Jews. For, in the eyes of Karl Marx, Judaism was the spirit of commerce. Ending discrimination against the Jews on the grounds of religion would give them political equality but would do nothing to solve the problem of why religion existed in the first place, which was due to social inequality. Religion was the expression of man's alienation under the conditions of capitalism and true emancipation would mean the end of the capitalist system. It was here that the two parts of Marx's argument joined up. 'Emancipation from huckstering and from money, that is from practical, real Judaism, would be the same as the self-emancipation of our age.' By this he meant that the spirit of the Jews, commerce or monetary exchange, had become the dominant form of transaction in society. And for Marx, just as for Hegel, Judaism represented the alienation of man from nature. In Marx's version, though, it was money exchange, the essence of practical Judaism, that alienated man from his labour. Religion was thus the expression of alienation, and the ending of alienation by revolution would put paid to religion. Hence the Jewish Question would be resolved once and for all.[20]

There is a great deal of speculation about the deeper, possibly unconscious motives, for Marx's essay on the Jewish

Question. What is certain is the effect it had on how socialists came to perceive 'the Jew'. Marx, like his philosophical predecessors, saw no intrinsic value in Judaism or the continuation of Jewish life. Intellectuals from Voltaire, through Kant, to Hegel could see no point in the Jews and anticipated their assimilation and disappearance once they dropped their stubborn resistance to reason (implicitly synonymous with Christianity). In Marx's theory, however, all religion was an outcome of an unjust society and would evaporate once social relations were equalised. But there was an extra reason why the Jews would vanish after the revolution: because Jews were hucksters in the interstices of the economy and Judaism was synonymous with the spirit of commerce. Marx's impact on socialist attitudes towards the Jews was manifold. First, he solidified and gave a scientific patina to the identification of Jews with finance and commerce, giving enduring life to a mythic representation of 'the Jew'. Second, he undermined the validity of Jewish life by reducing it to huckstering and exploitation. Finally, he defended Jewish rights in the short term but predicted that the Jews would eventually liquefy. So, for Orthodox Marxists the defence of the Jews would always be quixotic. What was the reason for these exertions and risks if the Jews were interlocked with capitalism and doomed by the revolution?

The paradox and tragedy of Marx's position is that it became doctrine at roughly the same time as other socialists were sensing the danger of anti-Jewish currents and noting that these animosities had an aetiology and a life quite independent from rationally explicable social or economic processes. One of the first to realise this was Moses Hess

(1812–75), a child of the French Revolution and Jewish enlightenment. He was born in Bonn to Jewish parents who enjoyed freedom under French rule from the 1800s until 1815. Thereafter he tasted the bitterness of discrimination and exclusion but remained a Jew, perhaps thanks to the schooling in Judaism he received from his pious grandfather. Hess drifted into the revolutionary movement in France in the 1830s, wrote socialist tracts, and collaborated with Marx on a number of significant left-wing publications. Hess's socialism was partly rooted in Jewish traditions of social justice and he unsettled Marx by referring to the Hebrew prophetic writings as a source. Their paths diverged not least because Hess became increasingly concerned about anti-Jewish trends in European politics and felt the tug of solidarity with other Jews. After the failure of the 1848 revolution in Germany, Hess settled in France from where he observed French expansion into the Levant and the rise of Italian nationalism. In 1862 he published *Rome and Jerusalem*, an extraordinary synthesis of Jewish values, socialist goals, and aspirations for the restoration of a Jewish homeland in Palestine.

Hess began by proclaiming his identity with the Jewish people. He trumpeted Jewish ideals, which he saw as an inspiration for social justice, and not to be lightly renounced. In any case, he observed that assimilation was not succeeding, while anti-Jewish animosity was taking on a new, irremediable character: 'The German ... objects less to the Jews' peculiar beliefs than to their peculiar noses'. The Jew who sought to blend in was despised 'for disowning his race because the heavy hand of fate oppresses it'. Instead, Jews ought to recognise themselves to be a nation and use their nationality as a vehicle for their historic mission to bring social justice to mankind. This could only be accomplished if the Jews had their own country: until then the Jewish masses would be beyond reform and Jewish energies would be dissipated. 'With the Jews, more than with any other nations which though oppressed, yet live on their own soil, all political and social progress must necessarily be preceded by national independence. A common, native soil is a primary condition if there is to be introduced among the Jews better and more progressive relations between capital and labour.' Hess argued that in view of the deepening French involvement in the Levant and Egypt the Jews might obtain French patronage for a return to Palestine and there build an ideal society. The Jewish homeland would serve as a platform for their role in the revolutionary regeneration of society: 'The Jewish people will participate in the great historical movement of present day humanity only when it will have its own fatherland.'[21]

Rome and Jerusalem sold few copies and Hess died a little-known figure. Yet he was uncannily prescient about the dangers of racism in Germany and outlined the core of what became socialist Zionism. His warnings had little resonance amongst the German Jewish bourgeoisie because they were bent on assimilation and sensed that liberal nationalism in Germany was working in their favour. Hess had little purchase amongst Jewish workers who, where they existed at all, were concentrated in Eastern Europe. What he wrote only made sense twenty years later when social and economic forces that could not have been predicted actually came into alignment as he suggested.

4 Social democracy and the Jews

The life of Ferdinand Lassalle (1825–64) was more typical of the trajectory followed by Jewish socialists at this time. He came from a Jewish reform background in Breslau and was a characteristic product of the Jewish Enlightenment. From a youthful engagement with Hegelianism, Lassalle moved into the revolutionary movement in the 1830s, worked with Heine in France, and took a dramatic part in the 1848 revolution in Germany. In the 1860s he embarked on a campaign to organise German workers into an electoral movement, anticipating the efforts of Marx and Engels. He died in a duel over a lover. His legacy was two-fold. He was a central figure in the development of social democracy in Germany and supplied the first example of a Jew in a position of leadership. But his ambivalence towards his Jewish origins and his tendency to lambast Jewish capitalists set an unfortunate precedent for subsequent German socialists of all backgrounds.[22]

Thanks to the pioneering efforts of men like Lassalle, by 1890 the German Social Democratic Party [SPD] was the largest and best organised working class political movement in the world and seemed poised to take power democratically. In normal circumstances the SPD's attitude towards the Jews would have been a minor chapter in this story of political success. But the tragic turn in German history has made the SPD's position on the 'Jewish Question' a subject of intense historical scrutiny – and much anguish. From the 1890s onwards, Germany was also the arena for the first mass-based anti-semitic parties and the failure of the SPD to check anti-semitism and, ultimately, its collapse in the face of the National Socialism in the 1930s have posed hard questions about socialism and the Jewish Question.

The rise of anti-semitic parties that were also explicitly anti-socialist forced the SPD leadership to address the 'Jewish Question'. This was an acutely uncomfortable process even for a party that prided itself on its freedom from prejudice. Many SPD leaders and its chief thinkers, notably Karl Kautsky (1854–1938), were Jews. Between 1893 and 1918, fifteen out of seventeen non-baptised Jewish deputies in the Reichstag sat for the SPD. Whereas the Liberals courted Jewish votes but caused intense embarrassment by selecting Jewish converts as Reichstag candidates, the SPD accepted Jews without differentiation. However, party organs frequently attacked Jewish capitalists as Jews and pandered to popular prejudice. The leadership was nervous about tackling anti-semitism head-on for fear of alienating working class voters who were viscerally anti-Jewish. Engels (1820–95), the doyen of the party till his death, tended to pardon working class anti-semitism as primitive anti-capitalism and repeated Marx's line that the Jews would anyway disappear along with capitalism. Engels argued that anti-semitism only appeared where capitalism was underdeveloped and in Jewish hands. Consequently, anti-Jewish animus would be eroded by the development and ramification of capital. The only reason for opposing anti-semitism and warning workers against it was that it occluded the class struggle. The rage of workers was diverted on to one target and missed the bigger class enemy: the bourgeoisie and the ruling class as a whole.[23]

Engels represents a persistent tendency on the Left to demean, excuse and marginalise anti-semitism. His analysis reflected a feeling of contempt or indifference towards Jews that was rooted in the Enlightenment, a sense that their existence and welfare were of little importance in the long run. Jews and Judaism were reduced to class phenomena. It was routinely believed that Jews were attacked for reasons of class, not due to deep-rooted religious or cultural misconceptions or racism. So the end of class struggle would bring the end of anti-semitism. Engels and his peers did not perceive that anti-Jewish feeling was autonomous from class issues, and they had no sense that the Jews were a collectivity which merited as much respect and defence of its human rights as any other.

The failings of the socialist approach were starkly exposed during the Dreyfus Affair. Although the quixotic Jewish socialist-anarchist Bernard Lazare (1865–1903) identified the fallacy of the case against Dreyfus and early on campaigned for a retrial, the appeals for support that he addressed to the French socialists fell on deaf ears. In 1898, the Confédération Générale du Travail issued a pamphlet that declared: 'We the Workers, constantly exploited, have no call to take part in this conflict between Jew and Christian! They are both the same, since they both dominate and exploit us!' It was only the socialist deputy Jean Jaurès who realised that the cause of

Dreyfus was linked to the cause of justice and democracy in France and was, therefore, a matter for the workers. [24]

Socialist responses to anti-semitism in Germany, too, were continually vitiated by the use of class as the sole category of social analysis and advocacy of Jewish assimilation. The SPD leader and propagandist August Bebel (1842–1913) famously dismissed anti-semitism as 'the socialism of fools'. He urged workers to resist the blandishments of the anti-semitic and Christian Socialist parties, but not for the sake of the Jews. In the statement on anti-semitism that he drafted for the SPD conference in 1893 he reduced anti-semitism to 'the discontent of certain bourgeois strata, who find themselves adversely affected by the development of capitalism and are, in part, destined to perish economically as a result of these trends'. Bebel characterised the Jews as a 'race', condemned their alleged apartness, and predicted that they too would disappear thanks to the force of progress. In *Rasse und Judentum* [Race and the Jews, 1914], an analysis of anti-semitism that became the gospel for German socialists, Kautsky wrote: 'it is only in the ghetto, as a condition of compulsory exclusion from their environment and deprived of their rights and surrounded by hostility, that Jews can maintain themselves among other peoples. They will dissolve, unite with their environment and disappear, where the Jew is regarded and treated as a free man and an equal.'[25]

The position of the Austro-Marxists is even more perplexing. Almost the entire leadership cadre of the Austrian Social Democratic Party was Jewish, and Vienna was one of the testing grounds for anti-semitic politics in the 1890s. Yet the party's inspirational leader Victor Adler

(1852–1918) asserted that hatred of Jews was no more than a symptom of crisis in the bourgeoisie. The Jews, he claimed, were no less a product of capitalism. So the conflict represented by anti-semitism was nothing to do with the workers. Adler proclaimed in 1889 that 'The Austrian workers desire neither "Jewish" nor "Christian" exploitation and nobody could ever mobilise them either for or against the Jews.' He advised that opposition to anti-semitism meant taking the side of one faction of the bourgeoisie against another. At the 1891 congress of the Second International, Adler even championed a resolution equating and condemning both anti- and philo-semitism. Adler's reluctance to challenge the rising tide of Jew-hatred may have been partly related to his unease about his own Jewish background: he converted to Christianity and was always trying to shake off Jewish associations. But it was by no means unique and cannot be reduced to personality alone.[26]

Because they operated in the multi-national Austro-Hungarian Empire, the Austro-Marxists also struggled with the questions of nationality and ethnicity, a self-evidently crucial phenomenon that had nevertheless always been a blind spot in Marxist doctrine. The Jewish-born Otto Bauer (1881–1938), one of the chief theoreticians of the Austrian SPD, devised an innovative way to embrace national struggles within class struggles inside the empire. In his pathbreaking 1907 book *The Question of Nationalities and Social Democracy*, he categorised the aspirant national groups, such as the Czechs, and explained how the achievement of national rights (within a democratic, federated entity) was essential for the fulfilment of socialist goals. Yet Bauer dismissed

Jewish demands for national rights or cultural autonomy in the region of Galicia (where 800,000 Jews lived), insisting instead on assimilation. He replicated Marx's slighting analysis of the Jews as little more than an outgrowth of exchange, doomed to disappear after the revolution, and blamed Jews for anti-semitism by suggesting that as long as they sought to preserve their identity they would arouse hostility. 'All attempts to artificially block assimilation and to cultivate inside Judaism an ideology opposing assimilation go against progress, are reactionary.'[27]

However, it would be a mistake to dismiss the anti-anti-semitism of social democracy as a whole and to read back into the 1890s the catastrophe of the 1930s. Even champions of Marxist orthodoxy like Kautsky were capable of reworking their doctrine. In the 1900s Kautsky condemned Zionism as a reassertion of Jewish 'separateness' and a form of bourgeois nationalism, but he recognised the achievements of the Jewish labour movement in Russia, England and the USA. He sympathised with its use of Yiddish and autonomous unions and parties to mobilise Jewish workers. Eduard Bernstein (1850–1932), the revisionist who transmuted doctrinaire revolutionary Marxist socialism into a gradualist electoral strategy, was moved by his contact with Jewish workers in London's East End in the 1890s. Bernstein came from an assimilated Jewish background and admitted that he absorbed negative attitudes towards Jews. He was one of the few SPD leaders to condemn its tolerance of anti-semitism even though he sympathised with comrades who saw it as a bridge to real socialism.[28]

Rosa Luxemburg (1871–1919) is often wheeled out as an

example both of the weakness of Marxist class analysis when confronted by elemental forces of nationalism and xenophobia, and of a Jewish socialist who sublimated her identity in the working class movement and blinded herself to the hatred that eventually destroyed her. (She was murdered by anti-semitic right-wing terrorists in Berlin.) Luxemburg was born in south-west Poland into a family shaped by the Jewish Enlightenment and made a career in the Socialist Democratic Party of Poland and Lithuania. She bitterly opposed Polish nationalism, even its socialist variety, and Jewish nationalism in all its forms. Her attitude towards anti-semitism was notorious. In 1910 she wrote: 'For the followers of Marx, as for the working class, *the Jewish Question as such does not exist*, just as the "Negro Question" or the "Yellow Peril" does not exist. From the standpoint of the working class, the Jewish question ... is a question of *racial hatred as a symptom* of social reaction, which, to a certain extent, is an indivisible part of all social elites based on class antagonism.' However, if her refusal to recognise the specificity of the Jewish case was a mistake, it was at least congruent with her mistaken attitude towards all national movements. Nor was Luxemburg's dogmatism reducible to Marxist blinkers because, as Kautsky and Bernstein showed, it was possible to recognise the danger of anti-semitism and applaud the Jewish working class struggle within a conventional Marxist framework.[29]

Luxemburg's harsh attitude towards specific Jewish issues was as much a product of her time and place as it was the consequence of Marxist dogma. By 1910, she was engaged in a four-cornered struggle for the allegiance of workers in Poland. There were Polish nationalists, Polish socialists, Polish internationalists (like herself) and parties of the national minorities within Poland, including the Bund – the General Jewish Workers' Party of Lithuania, Poland and Russia. It is to the Jews of Russia that we now turn.

5 Jews, socialism, and revolution in Eastern Europe

By 1900 the Russian Jewish population stood at around 5 million, mostly crammed into the Pale of Settlement in western Russia and Poland – an area to which Jews had been restricted since the 1770s. The Jewish population was overwhelmingly small-town and rural. Outside of a few industrial centres, such as Warsaw and Lodz, Jews were engaged in small manufacturing or trading and processing agricultural produce. The vast majority were Yiddish-speaking and religiously observant. However, since the 1830s and 1840s the reformist ideas of Moses Mendelssohn had percolated into Russian Jewry, giving rise to the *haskalah* – the East European version of the Jewish Enlightenment. The *haskalah*, assisted by the liberalising measures of the Tsarist regime in the 1860s, led to the emergence of a Russified Jewish bourgeoisie. These middle class Jews were half removed from traditional Jewish life, which they regarded with contempt, and half integrated into Russia society, which treated them with extreme caution. Doubly alienated and schooled to challenge authority by the *haskalah* literature they had absorbed, these Jews were natural recruits for the anti-authoritarian Populist movement.[30]

As a result, Jews were integral to the development of the revolutionary movement in Russia from its inception in the 1870s. Significant numbers of Jewish men and women, out of all proportion to their numbers in the general population, entered the ranks of the Populists – the seedbed of the Russian revolutionary movements. These Jews tended to come from *maskilik* backgrounds, that is, their parents were involved in the *haskalah*. A typical example of this early wave of recruits was Pavel Akselrod (1850–1925), who was a thread connecting Populism to Bolshevism and an influence on both Marx and Lenin. The first circles of Jewish Populists crystallised in the University of St Petersburg and the state-run rabbinical seminary at Vilna. The Vilna seminary propagated modern interpretations of Judaism that unintentionally undermined all sorts of traditional allegiances and fostered a phenomenal number of Jewish revolutionaries until it was shut down. One of its most famous alumni was Aron Liberman (1848–80). After his revolutionary activity in Vilna was exposed, Liberman fled from Russia to London's East End where, in 1878, he founded the first Jewish trade union in the world. Another alumnus, Abraham Cahan (1860–1951), went on to found the hugely influential Jewish socialist newspaper *Forwarts* in New York that at its peak sold 200,000 copies daily. However, Liberman and Cahan were exceptional in the early timing of their commitment to work amongst Jews.[31]

Until 1881, Jews in the three main incarnations of the revolutionary movement – the People's Will, the Land and Freedom Party, and Black Repartition – eschewed special attention to the plight of Jews and Jewish workers in Russia.

They were aware that Jews faced discrimination, but believed it would be alleviated through a successful regime change. Although they subordinated ethnic-religious ties, they nevertheless made a distinctively Jewish contribution to the revolutionary movements. Jewish activists were typically the leading organisers, technicians, and financial managers in the underground – all areas in which the children of the Russian Jewish professional bourgeoisie had accumulated experience. Jews also proved adept at terrorism and assassination. The involvement of a Jewish woman, Hesia Helfhand, in the successful plot to assassinate Tsar Alexander II led to a crisis that transformed the landscape of Jewish socialism and the relations between the Left and the Jews.[32]

Following the assassination of Alexander II in March 1881, and the detection of Jewish involvement, the Russian authorities fomented the idea that Jews were behind the revolutionary movement. The Interior Minister, N. P. Ignatiev, proclaimed that: 'Judaism was the natural breeding ground of subversion.' In the spring of 1881 a wave of anti-Jewish riots spread from the Ukraine across southern Russia and into Poland. The riots were not engineered by the regime, as was once thought. It was actually taken aback by the breakdown of law and order and feared that the disturbances marked the onset of a revolution. Nevertheless, Jews blamed the government for the lack of protection and suspected that violence on such a scale could only have occurred if it was officially inspired or condoned. Thousands of Jews fled the riot-torn districts and headed for ports and border crossings to escape the country. Russified Jews who had believed that Russia was following the path of Western Europe towards emancipation were bitterly disillusioned. Many turned from assimilation to new ideologies such as Jewish nationalism. Jewish revolutionaries were no less stunned. They were horrified that elements of the People's Will welcomed the mayhem as a step towards revolution while propagandists for the revolutionary cause validated popular claims that the Jews were parasites feeding off the peasantry and the urban poor.[33]

Akselrod reflected the shock of Jewish revolutionaries in an essay addressed to Jewish youth in early 1882. He recalled how many like him had put aside Jewish ties in order to work for the revolution, only to find their comrades urging on the rioters to an orgy of murder, rape and destruction aimed against the Jews. 'Indiscriminate destruction and violence against tens of thousands of Jewish families,' he wrote, 'has finally opened the eyes of the Jewish-socialist intelligentsia to its mistake'.[34]

Akselrod eventually helped to persuade the People's Will that the pogroms were not revolutionary and stayed in the movement, along with a majority of its Jewish activists. But significant numbers sheared off and re-evaluated their ideology and affiliations. Stung by the pogroms and the apparent rejection of Jewish revolutionaries, groups in Vilna and Minsk formed socialist circles amongst Jewish artisans who had formerly been ignored by the peasant-obsessed Populists. In 1893, Julius Tsederbaum (later known as Martov; 1873–1923) was sent into internal exile in Vilna, a city of which 40 per cent of the population was Jewish. Martov was a Russified Jew from a *maskilik* family who had entered revolutionary circles while a student and been converted to Marxism. In Vilna he discovered a large Jewish artisanal proletariat that was ripe for organisation: they held their first May Day strike the year he arrived. But first the Russified Jewish intellectual had to learn Yiddish in order even to communicate with the other Jews. By 1895, Martov was issuing propaganda in Yiddish and appealing to a specifically Jewish working class agenda. Martov and other Jewish socialists made a three-fold transition in the early 1890s. First, they learned Marxism and gave up utopian, terroristic Populism. Second, they abandoned the peasantry in favour of organising the urban artisans and proletariat. Third, they resolved to organise Jewish workers even if that meant activating ethnic and communal ties that had been allowed to shrivel and that were frowned upon by universalistic, mainstream Marxist socialists like Rosa Luxemburg.[35]

Between 1894 and 1897 the Jewish workers' movement grew rapidly and was at the forefront of a strike wave that impressed hardened revolutionaries. In 1897 Martov and other Jewish socialists formed the Bund, which they intended to function as no more than a Jewish branch of the Russian Social Democratic Labour Party (RSDLP). However, the Bund developed its own dynamic. Its leaders recognised that Jews faced specific discrimination and a double oppression – from the Russian authorities and Jewish employers. Because the Jewish population formed a compact mass in the Pale, they believed it warranted recognition as a national minority like the Poles and Baltic peoples. At its 1899 Congress, the Bund formally demanded not just equal rights for Jews as individuals but national rights as a minority in the Russian Empire. This decision was popular with the Jewish rank and file and helped the Bund fend off competition from the Zionists; but it set the movement on a collision course with the internationalist RSDLP led by Lenin, Plekhanov, Leon Trotsky, Akselrod and Martov. The conflict came to a head at the RSDLP congress held in the East End of London in 1903. Lenin refused to accept the Bund as a constituent element of the RSDLP if it pursued a nationalist agenda. Defeated in a vote, the Bund walked out. The Bund's departure upset the voting pattern on other issues. Martov and Trotsky found themselves at the head of a minority in opposition to other of Lenin's policies. This minority, the *mensheviks*, subsequently seceded and the RSDLP split into two factions, the majority comprising the *bolsheviks*. For the next fourteen years these factions in effect became separate and rival parties.[36]

Meanwhile the Bund went its own way. Between 1903 and 1905, it organised Jewish armed self-defence against pogroms. During the Russian Revolution of 1905–6 it coalesced in practical action with the RSDLP and suffered horrendous casualties in street battles with the police and army throughout the cities of the Pale. After the failure of the revolution, thousands of Bundists emigrated to England, the USA, South Africa and Palestine. But the party remained intact and recovered. In 1912 the weakened Bund rejoined the RSDLP on condition that its demand for national-cultural autonomy was recognised. By now the Bund was not only a powerhouse of industrial organisation: it was a dynamo of Yiddish culture. Through political and industrial action the Bund forged a proletariat; through its press and patronage of writers it fostered a modern, secular, socialist Jewish culture in Yiddish. However, its leaders knew that the ideological and practical base of the Bund was always fragile. It could not achieve a revolution alone and always depended on other class parties. Yet these parties were loath to cooperate and constantly poached each other's members. The demand for national-cultural autonomy sounded good and held the Zionists in check, but no one knew what it would entail in practice. While proclaiming internationalism and solidarity, the Bund knew that its very existence was a testimony to the apartness of the Jews and the difficulties of integration. Failing the promised revolution, it was locked in a vicious circle. Over the years, these tensions would test the Bund to destruction.[37]

6 Socialists and the Jewish labour movement

The anti-Jewish riots in Russia and the anti-Jewish legislation that followed triggered a wave of mass migration from the Tsarist Empire to Western Europe, America and South Africa. Between 1880 and 1914, about 2.5 million Jews migrated westward. Only a part of this migration was a direct result of the pogroms: most of it was economic migration. Jews had been leaving Russia and Poland steadily since the 1870s owing to the pressure of population on jobs and resources in the Pale. The riots, which were anyway confined to two periods in 1881–2 and 1903–06, were localised. In the first period, the north-west of Russia was unaffected, yet it was from here that the bulk of emigrants departed. Similarly, Galicia in Austria Hungary exported tens of thousands of Jews, but they left a region untouched by riots and in which Jews were full citizens. The pogroms and persecution in Russia, however, convinced millions of Jews that they could not expect a better life for themselves or their children under Tsarism and turned a steady trickle of migration into a tidal wave.[38]

The mass migration of East European Jews had a double impact on relations between Jews and the Left. First, it led to the formation of a large Jewish proletariat in cities such as Paris, London and New York. Second, it stimulated calls to restrict Jewish immigration and thus created a 'Jewish Question' for the Left in countries that had not seen one since the struggle for emancipation – if at all.[39]

Between 1880 and 1914, about 120,000 Jews settled permanently in England with many thousands more spending time in London, Leeds or Manchester while en route to America. They lived in the cheap slum districts, notably the East End of London, close to their places of work and were overwhelmingly concentrated in the traditional Jewish artisanal trades (clothing, footwear, and furniture making) and petty commerce.[40]

In England, voices were raised against mass Jewish immigration as early as 1884. East London MPs first raised the issue in Parliament in 1886. Between 1887 and 1892 the call for immigration restriction was led by Tory MPs. However, they attracted support from old craft unions which feared competition from Jewish artisans and also from some leaders of new model unions, notably Ben Tillet (1860–1943) and Tom Mann, of the Dockworkers' Union. The TUC debated 'alien' immigration in 1892, 1894 and 1895, and on each occasion passed resolutions calling for restriction against the influx of what they saw as cheap labour. This contradicted the labour movement's historic commitment to free trade and piqued the interest of Tory imperialists such as Joseph Chamberlain who had been urging protection in the form of tariffs on goods imported from outside the empire. Chamberlain knew that protection was unpopular with the working classes, who traditionally associated tariffs with high food costs and remembered that the Tory Party had fought to keep the Corn Laws which had prevented the importation of cheap corn and thereby increased the cost of bread. He was now able to argue that there was no sense in seeking protection against cheap labour entering the country if goods that were produced abroad by the very same cheap labour were allowed in without controls. Chamberlain thus saw working class animosity to immigration as a Trojan horse with which to smuggle protection into their camp. At his instigation, immigration restriction became a plank of the Tory party election appeal in 1895. Chamberlain's ploy, and the trades union response to Jewish immigration, worried Keir Hardie (1856–1915). He told the 1895 TUC that what workers needed was unemployment insurance and labour exchanges, not restriction of immigration. However, the Tories took heart from working class xenophobia in East London and successfully exploited the immigration issue in the 1900 General Election. The election resulted in the arrival in Parliament of a large cadre of Tory imperialist MPs who immediately demanded action against immigration. They won a royal commission that sat from 1902 to 1903 and came up with a report that proposed a variety of restrictionist measures. The debate over Jewish immigration coincided with a sustained economic slump and high unemployment. Many Tory MPs saw restriction as a cheap gesture to appease working class voters and pressed the government of A. J. Balfour to pass appropriate legislation. A bill to curb 'alien immigration' was introduced in 1904, but was so savaged by Winston Churchill and Charles Dilke, two leading Liberal MPs, that it had to be withdrawn. Balfour, who was convinced that restriction was essential, brought in a new bill in 1905. The Aliens Act was passed and came into force in January 1906.[41]

Immigration restriction split the English labour movement. The Social Democratic Federation, led by Henry Hyndman (1842–1921), was in favour of immigration control. The Socialist League, led by William Morris (1834–96) and Eleanor Marx (1855–98), defended unrestricted immigration and actively cultivated ties with the Jewish working class in East London. Jewish workers were not idle bystanders to the debate. Amongst them were men like Morris Winshevsky (1856–1932), a graduate of the revolutionary circle in Vilna. In 1884 he founded the *Polishe Yidl*, London's first Yiddish socialist newspaper, and in 1885 followed it with the longer lasting *Arbeter Fraynt*. Winshevsky was a guiding light in the development of the Jewish trades union movement in London until he left for America. He presided over the successful tailors' strike of 1889, the first mass industrial action by Jewish workers in London. But the gains made in 1889 did not last long. Jewish trades unions tended to be unstable because they operated in seasonal industries cursed by a high proportion of casual labour and out-workers who were nearly impossible to unionise. London was in any case a bleak terrain for trades unionists. Even so, by the 1910s the clothing, footwear and furniture trades featured a number of well-established Jewish trades unions affiliated with the British labour movement and serving to integrate Jews into the wider working class. This was a success and an unforeseen boon because it helped to counter the allegations that Jews were nothing but *homo economicus.*[42]

The formation of Jewish immigrant communities in British cities created a 'Jewish Question' for the Left in Britain. The issue of immigration had already caused tension; now labour leaders had to define a position regarding Jewish workers, their communities and their unions. Should the British labour movement support separate Jewish unions? Should it admonish workers who expressed hostility to the immigrants and cultivate solidarity with them? Or should it articulate the fear in sections of the working class that the Jews were swamping inner cities? Keir Hardie embodied these ambivalences. He opposed the Aliens Act, but proposed an amendment to enable the exclusion of immigrant strike-breakers. Tillet eventually dropped restrictionism and resolved that his trades union would help London Jews organise. 'We may not like you,' he reputedly said, 'but we will do our duty by you.' Throughout the Left, Jews were spoken of as 'aliens', a term that denoted the immigrants as unEnglish and unassimilable. Amongst their alleged unEnglish traits was the inability to understand fair play. They were accused of introducing sweating, of undercutting, and of taking the jobs of Englishmen. The reluctance of Jews to join English trades unions was ascribed to their 'individualism' rather then their lack of language skills. The instability of Jewish trades unions was taken by observers such as Beatrice Potter (1858–1943) as evidence of the ruthless desire of Jews to get ahead on their own. Potter (later Mrs Beatrice Webb and a founder of the Fabians) made her observations while acting as an investigator for William Booth's great study of London life and labour. She opined that Jews 'Have neither the desire nor the capacity for labour combination.' 'The love of profit distinct from other forms of money earning', was, she wrote, 'the strongest impelling force of the Jewish race'. Potter's prejudiced reportage was nothing unusual: it stemmed from pre-existing notions about Jewish behaviour that were embedded in the left by Voltaire, Fourier and their ilk.[43]

The Left in England, like the SPD, was not immune to 'rich Jew anti-semitism', either. During the Boer War, English socialists accused the government of pandering to Jewish gold mine owners in South Africa, the so-called 'Rand Lords'. In his attacks on British military action against the Boers, J. A. Hobson, a leading opponent of imperialism, complained that the Transvaal was under the sway of 'Jew power'. Struck by what he believed he had stumbled on during the Boer War, in his influential critique of imperialism Hobson singled out Jews as exemplars of international finance capitalism and suggested that they played a shadowy role in world affairs. Although Hilaire Belloc and G. K. Chesterton cannot be called men of the left, they helped to set the tone in left-wing circles in the Edwardian era by their muckraking journalism and exposure of financial corruption in business and government. Belloc and Chesterton constantly indulged in innuendo against Jews and often employed crude anti-semitic stereotypes in their writing and speeches. It was no accident that two of the most sensational scandals they unleashed, the Marconi Scandal and the India Silver Scandal, involved a number of prominent Jews. On the eve of the First World War, then, it was common on the Left in Britain to find Jews negatively coupled with both high finance and cheap, sweated labour.[44]

A similar dynamic was evident in the United States, which absorbed over two million Jewish immigrants. The weakness of organised labour in America forestalled any coherent opposition to the influx and, in any case, the doors were held open by powerful vested interests eager for unlimited cheap labour. But even though Jews formed powerful trades unions and established a major presence in local politics, in New York especially, the Left regarded their arrival with ambivalence. By 1900, half a million Jews were crammed into the Lower East Side of New York where they lived in grim tenements and toiled in grimmer sweatshops. Jews dominated the electorate of the 9th district, but the Socialist Party studiously ignored their needs and interests. The Russian, Polish and Romanian Jews who read the Yiddish press worried about 'old country' issues and the threat of immigration restriction, as well as bread and butter questions concerning wages, conditions of work and the provision of welfare. The Socialist Party's founder and candidate in 1904 and 1908 was Morris Hillquit (1869–1933), who was himself a Jewish immigrant. But Hillquit was afraid that if he addressed the agenda of the Jewish population he would be accused of being 'foreign' himself. In 1904 he even spoke up for the restriction of immigration by 'backward races'. As a result of his timidity and 'assimilationism' he repeatedly failed to gain what should have been a solid seat. In 1910, Meyer London (1871–1926) succeeded Hillquit as the Socialist Party candidate and things changed. London played up his Jewish immigrant roots and unashamedly addressed a range of Jewish immigrant concerns. He spoke out against the anti-Jewish measures in Russia and fought to maintain free immigration. London finally won the seat in 1914 and held it until 1922 – the only socialist in the US House of Representatives.[45]

7 Zionism and the Left

The pogroms that had sparked the development of Jewish socialism in Russia and led to the mass emigration that produced Jewish proletarian communities in western cities were also responsible for the crystallisation of modern Zionism and, ultimately, the emergence of socialist Zionism as a political force.

In 1881–2, a number of disillusioned Jewish Populists resolved that, since Russia had rejected them, they would emigrate to Palestine, the ancestral Jewish homeland, and there work on the land to found utopian socialist communities. The first waves of emigrants were not very successful as farmers and were only rescued by the beneficence of Baron Edmond de Rothschild. Meanwhile Theodor Herzl (1866–1904) published his manifesto for the modern Zionist movement, *The Jewish State*, in 1897. Herzl depicted the creation of a Jewish state as the solution to the 'Jewish Problem', that is, the persistence of anti-semitism and the apparent failure of assimilation. He identified part of the 'problem' as the involvement of Jews with the revolutionary movements, which further aggravated Jewish-Christian relations. Zionism, he claimed, would diminish anti-semitism by siphoning away surplus and unassimilable Jews from the Diaspora to their own country, where they would enjoy equality and freedom from the warping effects of hatred and the effort to appease it. Zionism would also wean alienated and discontented young Jews away from revolution. Herzl was a classic nineteenth-century liberal nationalist, who was capable of making progressive overtures to labour while at the same time adopting a fundamentally non-socialist stance.[46]

Herzl went on to found the World Zionist Organisation as a vehicle for achieving his vision. But he rapidly encountered dissenters, especially amongst Zionists with left-wing politics. Nahman Syrkin (1868–1924), a Russian Jew from an enlightened and Russified background, resented Herzl's deployment of Zionism as an antidote to Jewish socialism. In 1898 he published a book entitled *The Socialist Jewish State* (1898), which argued that the Jewish bourgeoisie alone could never restore the Jewish state, because such an enterprise in an undeveloped region would require central planning, mobilisation of the Jewish masses as workers, and social ownership of the land and natural resources. Syrkin's most powerful arguments were reserved for socialists and the Jewish Left, in particular. He agreed that Jew-hatred was a product of economic friction and inequality, and that antisemitism was used by reactionaries to transcend class divisions and create a false unity. Yet socialism alone could not solve the 'Jewish Question'. Socialists prescribed revolution followed by assimilation, but Syrkin insisted on the value of Jewish existence and the continuity of Jewish values of social justice. Moreover, Jews were doubly oppressed as workers and members of a religious-ethnic minority; they could not wait for the revolution and did not want to disappear afterwards. The only solution, therefore, was transfer to their own state where the class struggle could be waged untrammelled by false solidarities and the contradictions of class and ethnicity. Jews would then be able to join the struggle for world socialism.[47]

Syrkin founded the first socialist Zionist party – Poale Zion. Its members led the second and third waves of emigration to Palestine in 1903–14 and 1919–22 and were responsible for creating the infrastructure of a socialist state: collective farms, cooperatives, factories owned and run by the trades union movement, health and education services. The second wave of socialist Zionists were armed with a more sophisticated theory by the more rigorously Marxist thinker Ber Borochov (1881–1917). Ber Borochov tapped into the thought of the Austro-Marxists who were groping towards a socialist theory of pluralism that would allow socialists to advocate class struggle and the realisation of minority rights within the multi-national Austro-Hungarian Empire. From them Borochov drew the lesson that unrequited nationalism distorted and blunted class struggle, while only the working class could supply a nationalist leadership that eschewed reaction. He argued that only the Jewish working class would be able to carry Jewish nationalism forward, because they were the only element of the Jewish people with nothing to lose. Jewish capitalists would never show much interest in emigration to, or investment in, an undeveloped corner of the world such as Palestine. In other words, the very dynamics of capitalism compelled Jewish workers to assume the vanguard of Jewish nationalism and, in turn, dictated that the Jewish state would be a socialist state destined for integration into a new socialist world order.[48]

Zionism, however, incurred the wrath of both the main Russian social democratic movement and the Jewish Bund. It was denounced by Marxist socialists as a form of bourgeois deviationism, a distraction from the class struggle. Kautsky formulated the most potent and influential critique of Zionism that still resonates in the Left today. To Kautsky, the Jews were a religious group and not a people or a nation. They were essentially urban dwellers and had no business going to the land – least of all someone else's. Their fate and future was assimilation in Europe or wherever they lived. 'We have still not completely emerged from the Middle Ages as long as Judaism still exists among us,' he wrote. 'The sooner it disappears, the better it will be for society as well as for the Jews themselves.' Jewish nationalism only fostered a sense of apartness and actually aggravated Jewish/non-Jewish relations. 'Zionism', he maintained in *Rasse und Judentum*, 'meets anti-semitism half way in this striving, as well as in the fact that its goal is to remove all Jews from the existing states.' The opposition of the Bund was, if anything, more hyperbolic since the Poale Zion was competing directly for the same constituency in Russia and Poland. It was, of course, impossible for the Marxist left to foresee that world revolution would not come and that the removal of the Jews would, in the end, be the only way of saving them from catastrophe.[49]

8 Jews and the Left in the face of Fascism and Nazism

The First World War ushered in a disastrous period for the Jews of Europe. The intensification of nationalism inevitably drew attention to the anomalous status of the Jews, along with that of other ethnic-faith minorities. Defeat led to the collapse of Tsarist autocracy in Russia, but the revolution was seized by the Bolsheviks who proved no less intolerant of democracy and pluralism. The exigencies of war also brought forth the Balfour Declaration, which pledged the British government to facilitate the creation of a Jewish National Home in Palestine. But the Declaration owed much to the conviction that the Jews were a powerful world-wide force and, in turn, seemed to validate that perception.[50]

The Russian Revolution led to the complete emancipation of Russia's Jews. In the free elections for the Constituent Assembly in 1917, the vote amongst Jews for Jewish parties predominated over the vote for the Bolsheviks. But the attention of hostile observers fell on the substantial number of Jews who threw themselves into the service of the Soviet regime. Trotsky, Zinoviev, Kamenev and Radek, for example, were all of Jewish origin. At one point half the central committee of the Communist Party was Jewish. The high proportion of Jews in the upper reaches of the Bolshevik Party gave rise to the myth that 'the Jews' were behind the revolution and somehow inherently prone to Marxism. During the Russian Civil War, counter-revolutionary White officers circulated *The Protocols of the Elders of Zion*, a notorious forgery that purported to record a Jewish plan for world domination, as if it explained all that had occurred. The *Protocols* were picked up by British officers aiding the White armies and transmitted to London. In 1919 the first English version of the *Protocols* was published in the *Morning Post.* It attracted considerable attention and was soon selling well in book form under the title *The Causes of the World's Unrest.* Even Winston Churchill came to believe that Jews had to choose between two Jewish ideologies, one benign, and the other malign: Zionism or Bolshevism. The *Protocols* and the belief in an international Jewish conspiracy to overthrow the established order became received wisdom on the anti-socialist right.[51]

Heightened nationalism and xenophobia compromised the status of even the most assimilated Jews and left Jewish immigrants terribly exposed. In 1914, the British government passed a wartime Aliens Restriction Act terminating immigration, amongst other measures. In 1919, while in the grip of a xenophobic, anti-alien, anti-Bolshevik and anti-semitic hysteria, Parliament passed the Aliens Restriction (Amendment) Act. It permitted immigration officers, the police, magistrates and the Home Secretary to detain and deport without right of appeal any alien engaged in political or 'industrial' subversion, convicted of a crime, or found in breach of the alien registration rules. Hundreds of immigrant Jews were deported under these extraordinary powers, mostly while Sir William Joynson-Hicks was Home Secretary in the Conservative administration of 1924–9. Only a few Liberal and Labour MPs opposed the Act. One of them was Josiah Wedgwood (1872–1943), who became known as the champion of Jewish immigrants and other Jewish causes, including Zionism. Despite making sympathetic noises to the Anglo-Jewish community while in opposition, the Labour Party declined to revoke the Act when it held power in 1924 and 1929–31. It did, however, institute an appeals tribunal in 1929.[52]

The Red Scare that accounted in part for the 1919 Aliens Act took hold in the USA, too, where hundreds of Russian Jews were rounded up and deported in the so-called Palmer Raids. Emma Goldman (1869–1940) and Alexander Berkman (1870–1936), two leading socialist-anarchists, were amongst the most prominent victims. Goldman was deported to Russia where she became a scourge of Lenin's dictatorial tendencies. Ironically, in Russia itself the Bolsheviks were beginning the systematic destruction of Jewish communal life. Jewish sections of the Communist Party, the Evsekstiia, were set up to liquidate the Bund and the Zionist parties. Jews were granted national minority status in the USSR and a degree of cultural autonomy, but this became a liability once the regime embarked on the suppression of Jewish religious life and anything not congruent with Bolshevism. Nevertheless, Jews were permitted to establish collective farming settlements in which Yiddish was used, and in the 1930s Stalin even ordained the creation of a Jewish Sham 'autonomous region' in Birodidzhan, in remote Central Asia.[53]

Despite the ambiguous treatment of Jews in the USSR, the Communist Party continued to attract adherents in the west. Many Jews were attracted by its ideology. To others it was a shield against anti-semitism and the far right. For, along with the social democratic parties, the CP was the staunchest opponent of the anti-semitism and right-wing politics that were gaining influence and power all over Europe. Jews and the Left became locked in a fatal mutuality: the prominence of Jews in the Left attracted anti-semitism which only the Left was prepared to resist. To the right, the identification of Jews with Marxism and revolution was self-evident: Rosa Luxemburg was, along with the non-Jewish Karl Liebknecht, a leader of the Independent SPD; Ernst Leviné (1883–1919), Gustav Landauer (1870–1919) and Ernst Toller (1893–1939) ran the short-lived Bavarian Red Republic; Bela Kunn (1886–1939) was the leader of the equally short-lived Soviet regime in Hungary in 1919 (in which no less than 18 out of the 29 'peoples' commissioners' were Jewish); and Léon Blum (1872–1950) became Prime Minister at the head of the French Popular Front government in 1936. In England Emmanuel Shinwell (1884–1986), a firebrand on Red Clydeside, was held up as an example of the Bolshevik Jew undermining the British Empire. Right-wing anti-semitism and the ascent of the Nazis drove a generation of young Jews into the ranks of the Left. They comprised what one of them, Arthur Koestler, called the 'pink generation'. The acme and the most vivid illustration of the virtual synthesis between Jewish youth and the Left came during the Spanish Civil War. Over 8,000 Jews fought in the International Brigades in Spain, out of a total of 40,000 foreign volunteers.[54]

In Britain, the 'Battle of Cable Street' seemed to typify the situation in microcosm. In early October 1936, Sir Oswald Mosley, leader of the British Union of Fascists, threatened to march thousands of pro-Nazi Blackshirts through the Jewish districts of the East End of London. Left-wing Zionists and Jewish socialists prepared to stop them, although the Jewish communal leadership notoriously advised Jews to stay at home on the day of the march. Under pressure from Jewish members, the CPGB at the last moment cancelled a demonstration in Trafalgar Square in solidarity with the Spanish Republic and told its members to rally instead in the East End. Uniting under the slogan 'They Shall Not Pass', which was taken from the defence of Madrid against the Francoist forces, an estimated 100,000 people, including Jews, Irish dockworkers and East London trades unionists of all descriptions, blocked access to Whitechapel and Stepney. Although much romanticised and manipulated in retrospect, to Jews the role of the Left in the defence of Jewish people cemented bonds of loyalty. This loyalty bore fruit in 1945 when Mile End became the only British parliamentary constituency to elect a Communist member of parliament, Phil Piratin (1907–2001).[55]

Thanks to the Balfour Declaration and the Mandate for Palestine, during the interwar years Britain was uniquely entwined in the 'Jewish Question'. The Balfour Declaration was another outcome of the Great War that reconfigured relations between Jews and the Left. By and large, socialists in Britain welcomed the Balfour Declaration and British patronage of the Jewish National Home. Their position was influenced, first, by the eminence of socialist enterprise in Palestine. Jewish pioneers appeared to be exemplars of European socialism struggling to bring democracy and development to a benighted region still dominated by feudalism. It was this that impressed Ramsay MacDonald (1866–1937) when he visited the country in 1921. Recalling Tel Aviv in his 1922 pamphlet *A Socialist in Palestine*, the future leader of the first Labour government wrote: 'Whatever Labour can do by its own organisation is done without the intervention of the Capitalist, and if the sand on the one hand and the Moslem on the other give trouble, the heart of the Jewish worker is buoyant. He has left a bad old world behind: he is to be the creator of a new one.' The second factor endearing Zionism to the British Left was a negative one. During the early 1920s, Zionism and British involvement in Palestine were the target of a ferocious right-wing campaign in the press and parliament which harped on about bare-legged Jewish Bolshevik women desecrating the soil of the Holy Land. What condemned Zionism in the eyes of Lords Northcliffe, Rothermere and Beaverbrook, as well as Tory die-hard MPs like Joynson-Hicks, only commended it to the likes of MacDonald and Wedgwood.[56]

However, this honeymoon was not to last. There were conflicting currents in the Labour Party with regard to Zionism and the tensions within the Zionist project inevitably brought them to the surface. In 1929 the Labour Government had to contend with a serious outbreak of anti-Jewish rioting in Palestine. A commission of inquiry despatched by Lord Passfield (1859–1947), the Colonial Secretary, reported that Palestinian Arabs were alarmed by the volume of Jewish immigration and the extent of Jewish land purchases. In

1930, Passfield issued a White Paper proposing the restriction of Jewish immigration and the curtailment of land buying. The White Paper caused a storm of protest throughout the Jewish world. Its appearance coincided with a by-election in Whitechapel, a constituency with a high proportion of Jews amongst the electorate. The Liberal Party exploited the backlash against the White Paper by selecting as its parliamentary candidate Barnett Janner, a Jewish communal figure who was well known as a Zionist. Janner only narrowly missed capturing the seat after a rowdy campaign. Ernest Bevin (1881–1951), leader of the Transport and General Workers' Union, was himself subject to barracking at a mass meeting in the Whitechapel Art Gallery in November 1930 – an experience which he may have recalled when responsible for Palestine as Foreign Secretary in 1945–8. Within a few weeks the Prime Minister, Ramsay MacDonald, intervened personally to scrap the White Paper.[57]

During the 1930s the threat of Fascism and the pervasiveness of anti-semitism softened socialist antipathies to Zionism. Léon Blum joined a pro-Zionist labour group; Eduard Bernstein, the ideologue of German social democracy, re-evaluated his position and aligned with Poale Zion; and even Trotsky wrote tepidly about Jewish nationalism. Sympathy for the Jews was heightened by the ordeal of wartime and news of the Nazi extermination campaign. The labour movements in the USA and Britain were distinctive in receiving information about the 'Final Solution' somewhat earlier than other sections of the community and acting on the news with greater alacrity. This was largely due to the strong ties between the Bund and international labour bureaux in America and England. In occupied Europe itself, socialists and communists consistently offered more than the usual degree of support to Jews going underground or forming resistance groups. In the Soviet Union, from mid 1942 onwards partisan groups under Red Army control were instructed to assist Jews escaping ghettos and camps. In France, however, the CP resistance was so worried about being tarred as 'Jewish' that it segregated the Jews in separate units. Jews who entered the ranks of the Communist underground responded to the anxiety by virtually effacing their Jewish identity.[58]

In Britain, sympathy for the plight of the Jews in the form of pro-Zionism gained such force in the labour movement that in 1944 the Labour Party Annual Conference actually proposed transferring indigenous Arabs out of Palestine to enable the formation of a Jewish state. In power, however, national interest determined otherwise. Ernest Bevin's policy of restricting Jewish immigration to post-war Palestine, retaining it as a military base under British control, and preserving the territorial integrity of Palestine as an alternative to partition, disappointed Jews within and beyond the Zionist movement. Over 100,000 survivors of Nazi persecution and genocide languishing in miserable Displaced Persons' camps clamoured to get away from Europe to Palestine, but the Foreign Secretary of a famously pro-Zionist party sent the Royal Navy to intercept Jewish 'boat people' trying to reach Palestine and ordered that they be deported to camps on Cyprus and Mauritius or, even worse, back to camps in Germany. It was one of the most controversial and ugly chapters in the story of the British Left and the Jews.[59]

9 The Left and the Jews from post-war to Cold War

While reified ideological positions that had crystallised decades earlier continued to over-determine relations between Jews and the Left, the period from 1945 to 1989 registered several contingent changes that were of epochal significance. Most obviously, and tragically, the Nazi persecution and mass murder of Europe's Jews had destroyed the Jewish proletariat that provided the demographic base of Jewish socialism. With the exception of the far right, political activists of all shades learned from the catastrophe of Nazism that anti-Jewish discourse was toxic. The mainstream social democratic Left in Western Europe and North America purged itself of any traces of 'rich-Jew anti-semitism' and guarded against its recurrence. Jews, on the other hand, could not forget that the promise of revolution and fraternal solidarity had failed to save Jews from destruction. Although the Red Army and the USSR had borne the brunt of the struggle that eventually destroyed Hitler, and so won the undying gratitude of a generation of Jews, the post-war treatment of Jewish populations in the Soviet bloc along with attitudes towards Jewish nationalism further soured Jewish–Left interactions.[60]

During the Second World War, Stalin had allowed the formation of a Jewish Anti-Fascist Committee (JAFC) that was intended to build support in Britain and the USA for a second front. But Stalin was never comfortable with a distinctive Jewish socialist movement and at the same time that he was patronising the Jewish Anti-Fascist Committee he was ordering the shooting of Bundist leaders who had escaped from Nazi-dominated Poland to the Soviet Union. However, the existence of the JAFC legitimated a particularistic Jewish agenda in the USSR and for several years Jewish socialists and Yiddish writing again flourished in Russia. Even more surprisingly, Stalin swung the USSR behind the Zionist movement in its fight against the British in Palestine in 1946–8. The USSR was the first state to recognise Israel *de jure* in May 1948, and through its Czechoslovak proxy supplied the embattled state with arms and military training facilities. In summer 1948 Golda Meir visited Moscow as a representative of the Jewish state and was acclaimed by local Jews. These manifestations of double loyalty, together with disappointment that Israel had adopted a non-aligned foreign policy, caused Stalin to rethink his own policy. In late 1948, the JAFC was suppressed and its leading members were shot. Between 1949 and 1952, a wave of officially promoted anti-Zionism swept through the Soviet bloc, culminating in a series of show trials against 'rootless cosmopolitans'. Zionism was now routinely depicted in official organs as the stalking horse of Western and American interests.[61]

While the USSR never reversed its recognition of Israel, it invested heavily in Arab nationalism from the mid 1950s onwards. This development thwarted any rapprochement between Israel and the USSR after Stalin's death and helped to drive Israel into the camp of the Western powers, confirming the suspicions of the Soviet leadership. While Jews in the USSR were spared serious persecution thanks to Stalin's demise, they lived under a blanket of suspicion. They remained identified formally as Jews, but any expression of Jewish culture was proscribed. In effect, they were subjected to forced assimilation. The show trials and the repression of Jewish life were a shock to Jewish socialists outside the USSR, and helped to detach many Jewish Communists from Moscow. Soviet-inspired anti-Zionism after the 1967 Middle East war and a new wave of 'anti-Zionist' purges in eastern bloc countries (notably in Poland) speeded the process by which Jews came to see the Soviet and orthodox Marxist Left as nothing but inimical to Jewish interests.[62]

Meanwhile, social change elsewhere in the Jewish diaspora and the establishment of the State of Israel inexorably altered the mutual perceptions and interactions of Jews and the Left. During the 1950s and 1960s, the descendants of the proletarianised Jewish immigrants moved from inner city slums to the suburbs and entered white collar and professional employment. While these middle class Jews in France, Britain and the USA continued to vote to the left of their economic interests, there was a growing tension between their agenda and that of the mainstream left, not to mention the far left. For a while this divergence was masked by the continued salience of Jews who had entered the Left during the 'pink decade' of the 1930s, particularly in the United States where the anti-American witch-hunts led by Senator Joe McCarthy constantly spotlighted Jewish figures. Dozens of Jews in Hollywood, like the film directors Abraham Polonsky and Carl Foreman, were blacklisted or forced to migrate to Europe. Most notoriously, Ethel and Julius Rosenberg were sent to the electric chair for espionage on behalf of the USSR, the only spies convicted at this time to be executed for their crimes. On the other hand, for over a decade there was almost a honeymoon between the Jewish state and the social democratic left. Israel offered a new image of the Jew as farmer, worker and citizen-soldier, striving to realise a social democratic dream in the Middle East that was hugely attractive to socialists who had been politicised during the inter-war years and who had lived through the Nazi period. Many of them remained supporters of Israel long after the country had ceased to be an island of egalitarianism and a model democracy in a sea of reactionary regimes.[63]

The emergence of anti-colonialism and anti-imperialism as central planks in the ideology and activism of the New Left in the 1960s turned Israel from being an asset into a liability for Jewish socialists. Every Communist party in Western Europe supported the Arab cause in the run-up to the 1967 war and afterwards. In France, the Communist daily *Humanité* published articles that questioned whether Israel even had a right to exist. The French CP newspaper imported from the USSR the new line that Zionists and Nazis had collaborated during the Second World War, that Zionism was racist and no better than Nazism. For *Humanité* there was a direct connection between the national liberation struggle of the Vietnamese and the conflict in the Middle East: 'The Middle East crisis and the American intervention in Vietnam are inter-connected. This cannot be denied. The only difference is that while in Vietnam the Americans intervene directly, they cleverly use the Israeli ruling classes in the Middle East to fight Arab governments whose intention of controlling their own oil incurs American displeasure' (7 June 1967). The CP position was denounced by Jean-Paul Sartre, who recalled the recent genocide against the Jews: 'Hence we are allergic to anything that bears even the slightest resemblance to anti-semitism: a proposition to which many Arabs would reply: "We are not anti-semitic, we are anti-Israel," and no doubt they are right: but can they alter the fact that for us Israelis are also Jews? ... The idea that the Arabs could destroy the Jewish state and drive its inhabitants into the sea is anathema unless I am a racist.'[64]

The attitude of the New Left towards Israel was crucial to the mutual repositioning that occurred in Jewish communities and on the Left. The New Left embraced Third World struggles and saw anti-Zionism as a necessary correlative of anti-imperialism, anti-Americanism and support for national liberation movements. The symbiosis is neatly illustrated by a chant at a rally of Students for a Democratic Society (SDS) on an American campus in 1968: 'Ho, Ho, Ho Chi Minh, *Al Fatah* will win'. The SDS, whose leadership overwhelmingly comprised Jewish students from elite universities – students such as Richard Flaks, Al Haber and Todd Gitlin – made common cause with Black radicals, including the Black Panthers and Black Muslims. Indeed, African-American militancy introduced a fresh element to the dynamic of Jews and the Left. The new ethnic politics in the USA, soon to be echoed in Europe, cut across and disrupted old allegiances. In 1968, a New York teachers' strike degenerated into an ugly struggle between Blacks and Jews for the patronage of the local state. This was the beginning of the movement, culminating in affirmative action policies, that would pit Jews against Blacks and rupture an historic alliance forged during the civil rights struggles from the 1930s through to the 1960s.[65]

Social change played its part, too. Several leading Black Power activists, notably Eldridge Cleaver and Malcolm X, expressed the resentment Blacks felt against the role of Jews in the economy of the Black 'ghettos'. This feeling of exploitation conjoined with Black affinities for Third World struggles. The resulting blend is illustrated in a speech by Malcolm X from 1964: 'These people conduct their business in Harlem, but live in other parts of the city. They enjoy good housing. Their children attend good schools and go to colleges. This the Negroes know and resent. These businessmen are seen by the Negroes in Harlem as colonialists, just as the people of Africa and Asia viewed the British, the French and other businessmen before they achieved their independence.' In 1968, Cleaver denounced a Jewish judge trying a case involving a Black Panther with the words, 'we'll make a coalition with the Arabs, against the Jews, if that's the way you want it'.[66]

Yet when it came to the Jews, the positions adopted by the New Left were not so 'new' after all. An article in the London *Socialist Leader* in October 1970 attacked 'Zionism – Religious Fascism'. According to the article, typical of its genre, Zionism was the product of Judaism: 'It was primarily in pursuance of, and for the eventual fulfilment of, such prophecies that Zionism was founded at the turn of the century, with the express purpose of restoring the "Chosen Race" to Israel, the "Holy Land", Palestine, that Jehovah the God of the Jews had given to their remote ancestors but from which they had been expelled by Roman pagan invaders in AD 70 exactly 19 centuries ago.' Since religion was ephemeral and invalid this was hardly a good reason to create a state. 'The real paradox inherent hitherto in the current state of Israel is that it was actually founded for a different purpose from which its present leaders advocate. Currently, we have the still further paradox of a Zionist racial state claiming the sympathy and support as a "National Home" for the Jews...'(10 October 1970).

Social change, ethnic politics, and the increasing importance of Israel to Jewish identity drove a wedge between Jews and socialism. The New Left in particular appeared to threaten not only the economic interests of middle class Jews but what was increasingly becoming a central tenet of their identity: Israel. Partly in response, Jews drifted towards the right during the 1970s and 1980s. They were actively courted, too, by politicians such as Margaret Thatcher in England and Ronald Reagan in the USA. The mainstream right tried to shed its reputation for anti-Jewish sentiment, not least by espousing a strong pro-Israel line. Jewish political realignment heightened the negative attitude of left wing activists, fostered by a sense of betrayal that Jews should now consort with the political right. A vicious cycle was set in motion.[67]

The New Left maintained the anti-fascist and anti-antisemitic traditions of the old left, but it also perpetuated the traditional left-wing unease with the continued existence of the Jews as a people or nation. While vehemently defensive of the rights of Jews as citizens, it rejected the rights of Jews as a collectivity. Nor was the resistance to anti-semitism unconditional. Since New Leftists deemed that anti-semitism was rooted in social inequality, they decreed that it would disappear with the creation of a just society. According to this diagnosis, Jews had to be committed to the revolution to merit solidarity. Yet the revolution would spell not only the end of racism, but the evaporation of the Jews.

The contradictions within the New Left and the hard left, to which it was giving shape, were spelled out graphically in Britain in the anti-racism campaigns of the mid-1970s. The Anti-Nazi League mounted the most effective challenge to the far-right National Front, but the ANL was dominated by Socialist Workers Party activists, whose doctrinaire extension of anti-racism to anti-Zionism repelled many Jews. As a consequence, the anti-racist movement split. The same tensions were evident in London in the mid 1980s when the GLC under Ken Livingstone attempted to pursue an ethnic politics that would engage Irish, Black, and Asian Londoners. This involved espousing or endorsing anti-Israel positions which alienated the Jewish communal leadership. The GLC attempted to balance its ethnic politics by supporting the Jewish Socialist Group (JSG), a small though vibrant neo-Bundist group that was anti-Zionist. But the militant secularism and anti-Zionism of the JSG was discordant with the largely religious and pro-Israel identity of mainstream Jews in the capital and appeared highly anachronistic in view of the fate of the Bund under the Nazis and Soviets. Jews welcomed the anti-racism of the GLC, but the connection it made with a failed Jewish politics and anti-fascism of the

1930s and 1940s was perceived as arcane. To most middle class Jewish Londoners it seemed preposterous, even offensive, that the promise of socialist revolution would be offered as a palliative for regular attacks on Israel.[68]

The gap between Jews and the Left was widened by the vehemence of anti-Zionism in the late 1970s and 1980s. Although the mainstream social democratic left supported Israel's right to exist even while it criticised aspects of Israel's policies, the far left felt no such restraints. In 1975 the UN, at the behest of the USSR and its allies, pronounced Zionism a form of racism and thereby gave left-wing anti-Zionists a powerful new weapon for their critical armoury. Working with this premise, Trotskyite and Maoist groups in Britain used the National Union of Students policy of 'No platform for racists' to ban Jewish student societies that were branded Zionist and therefore racist. Throughout the mid and late 1970s Jewish students resisted this onslaught with the support of the Broad Left, comprising Communists and Labour Party students. But several generations of Jewish graduates emerged from this ideological cauldron with an undifferentiated suspicion of the Left.[69]

The alienation of Jews was deepened by the wave of anti-Zionist propaganda and activism that followed the Israeli invasion of Lebanon in 1982. For years, Soviet-inspired propaganda had depicted Zionism as a form of racism and asserted that, as such, it was no different from Nazism. The suggestion of an ideological affinity between Zionism and Nazism led to the accusation that Zionists and Nazis had collaborated. This was a form of Holocaust denial and also presupposed a vast worldwide Jewish conspiracy. But during the 1980s the fantasy took hold in swathes of the Left. Its centrality and tenacity was revealed by the controversy in Britain over the play *Perdition*, written by the Trotskyite TV-dramatist Jim Allen and directed by Ken Loach. *Perdition* laid out every aspect of the alleged Nazi–Zionist collaboration: the conspiracy by Zionist Jews to send their own people to the gas chambers so as to obtain recompense through the creation of Israel, and the plot to cover up their foul deed. The script was laced with anti-semitic tropes, yet, when the play was pulled by the management of the Royal Court Theatre, it became a cause célèbre for intellectuals and activists of the far left. On radio and TV, Loach and Allen repeatedly condemned the 'Zionist lobby' for suppressing the truth about Nazi–Zionist collusion. The writer and broadcaster Michael Ignatieff commented that in so doing, the defenders of the play were 'pandering to the latent antisemitism that is still a factor in the modern world'.[70]

Between 1950 and 1990, the mainstream left in Europe and North America defended Jewish rights against anti-semitism and neo-Nazism. It contested the suppression of human rights in the Soviet bloc, specifically the repression of Zionism and the prevention of Jewish emigration to Israel. Social Democrats welcomed Israeli politicians of the left in the Socialist International and supported Israel's existence, even if they called for a withdrawal from the land occupied by Israel in the June 1967 war. Jews remained prominently involved with the centre left. There were dozens of Jewish Labour MPs in the British parliament from 1945 to 1979. American Jews were the biggest and most consistent financial backers of the Democratic Party and repeatedly voted to the left of anything warranted by their income or social status. The regimes in South Africa and Argentina automatically held Jews in suspicion: the old conflation of Jew with communist lived on. As Nelson Mandela has repeatedly acknowledged, Jews played a role in the ANC struggle that was massively out of proportion to their numbers in the white population. Denis Goldberg was only one of many Jews in the ANC who shared the dangers of the struggle against apartheid. In 1963 he was imprisoned along with four other whites involved with Mandela in the Rivonia underground cell. All four of Goldberg's fellow-prisoners were Jewish. Goldberg later recalled that at the start of each new day in prison he heard the guard walk along the cell block, saying as he passed one door after another, 'Morning Jew, morning Jew, morning Jew'.[71]

10 The Left and the Jews since the end of the Cold War

Since early 2001, Jewish communal organisations, institutions monitoring anti-Jewish currents, and various commentators have identified a 'new anti-semitism'. Several reports and observers have connected this 'new anti-semitism' with the Left. The 'new anti-semitism' has certain key ingredients, all of which actually echo traditional anti-Jewish themes. It is commonly alleged that Jews possess enormous financial power that is translated into political power. This is achieved through the funding of political parties, in what amounts to buying influence and then retaining it by the threat of cutting off funds – a form of blackmail. 'Jewish power' is held to be irresponsible, unaccountable and exercised behind the scenes: it is the work of a conspiracy or a cabal. The Jewish conspiracy is international and embraces London, Washington, New York and Jerusalem. As a result of hidden influences, US and British foreign policy is driven not by national interests but by Jewish interests, notably the service of Israel. The defence of Israel entails the defence of a regime committing war crimes that are on a par with those committed by the Nazis.[72]

There is evidence to support the contention that segments

of the Left in Britain and elsewhere in Europe are playing a distinctive role in the dissemination of this anti-Jewish discourse. Much of this evidence comes from statements or articles relating to the Israel/Palestine conflict, a clash of national aspirations roiled by international geo-politics, about which there are real and urgent differences of opinion. So it is important to stress that criticism of Israeli government policy (as against denial of Israel's right to exist) is perfectly legitimate when it is expressed in language that does not intentionally or unintentionally use or echo long-established anti-Jewish discourse, characterising Jews inside Israel or in the Jewish diaspora as singularly wealthy, powerful, conspiratorial, treacherous and malign.

On 14 January 2002, the *New Statesman* [NS] weekly magazine appeared with a cover design depicting a golden star of David piercing a Union flag. The cover was meant to dramatically complement the cover story, entitled 'A kosher conspiracy'. This article, by Dennis Sewell, asserted: 'That there is a Zionist lobby and that it is rich, potent and effective goes largely unquestioned on the left. Big Jewry, like big tobacco, is seen as one of life's givens. Wealthy Jewish business leaders, acting in concert with establishment types and co-ordinated by the Israeli embassy, have supposedly nobbled newspaper editors and proprietors, and ensured that the pro-Palestinian position is marginalized both in news reporting and on the comment pages.' Sewell gave evidence of journalists apparently being 'nobbled' by proprietors such as Conrad Black, who is 'married to Barbara Amiel, the enthusiastic Zionist'; by *éminences grise* like Lord Weidenfeld, who breakfasts with Peter Hain MP; by the

Board of Deputies of British Jews; by Bicom, a pro-Israel lobby group; and by the Israeli Embassy. He concluded ironically that: 'The truth is the "Zionist lobby" does exist, but it is a clueless bunch.' The article following Sewell's, by John Pilger, stated that the Prime Minster, the Rt Hon. Tony Blair MP, 'shamelessly appointed a friend Michael Levy, a wealthy Jewish businessman who had fundraised for New Labour, as his "special envoy" in the Middle East, having first made him Lord Levy'. Pilger listed Lord Levy's Jewish communal affiliations, and mentioned his house and business in Israel, and the fact that his son worked for the Israeli Ministry of Justice. This, he remarked with heavy sarcasm, 'was the man assigned by Britain's prime minister to negotiate impartially with Palestinians and Israelis'. Pilger compounded the picture of a lopsided British policy by citing recent British arms sales to Israel and support for Israel's campaign against the Palestinians (NS, 14 January 2002).

The cover and the content of this *New Statesman* outraged Jews and many socialists like David Triesman, general secretary of the Labour Party, who wrote to the weekly in condemnation. In the *New Statesman* issue of 11 February 2002, Peter Wilby, the editor, admitted that he 'got it wrong'. 'The cover was not intended to be anti-semitic; the *New Statesman* is vigorously opposed to racism in all its forms. But it used images and words in such a way as to unwittingly create the impression that the *New Statesman* was following an anti-semitic tradition that sees the Jews as a conspiracy piercing the heart of the nation.' And yet, a few weeks later, the NS carried an article by Andrew Stephen on the power of the Jewish lobby in America: 'Why Israel gets an easy ride'. 'The

Jewish lobby', Stephen claimed, 'is simply too strong for any US politician, Republican or Democrat, to ignore.' Stephen listed some of the donors to Clinton's election campaign and traced links from the pro-Israel lobby group Aipac to the State Department. He concluded that 'The Bush administration – even including Colin Powell – has been neatly coerced into justifying Israel's ever mounting aggression as part of the worldwide war against terrorism' (NS, 8 April 2002).

In spring 2003, Tam Dalyell MP was interviewed about the Blair premiership for an article in *Vanity Fair* (June 2003). He was indirectly quoted by the writer, David Margolick, as saying that 'he thinks Blair is unduly influenced by a cabal of Jewish advisers. He mentions Mandelson, Lord Levy (Blair's chief fundraiser) and Jack Straw...' This aside drew the attention of other journalists who asked Dalyell if he stood by the claim that the prime minister was in the thrall of a 'Jewish cabal'. When offered the chance to backtrack or apologise, Dalyell repeated what he had been reported as saying.[73]

The notion that Jews comprise a powerful and coordinated international force was also expressed by Perry Anderson in his editorial article for the highly influential theoretical journal *New Left Review*, July–August 2001. In 'Scurrying towards Bethlehem' (pp. 5–30), Anderson engaged in a standard polemic against Zionism, but his argument strayed into territory that had nothing to do with criticism of Israel. He observed that whereas most colonial settler states originated when settlers left the motherland, this was not the case for Jews who emigrated to Palestine from a diaspora in which they were everywhere a minority. The Jews had corrected this anomaly, though, by engaging in a process of reverse colonisation and had taken over America so as to provide Israel with a supportive mother country after all. 'Entrenched in business, government and media, American Zionism has since the sixties acquired a firm grip on the levers of public opinion and official policy toward Israel, that has weakened only on the rarest of occasions. Taxonomically, the colonists have in this sense at length acquired something like the metropolitan state – or state within a state – they initially lacked' (p. 15).

The Nazi–Zionist connection repeatedly surfaced amongst left-wing intellectuals and parties. In April 2002, the poet, academic and self-proclaimed man of the Left Dr Tom Paulin was interviewed by the Egyptian paper *Al-Ahram*. He told the paper that Jewish settlers on the West Bank are 'Nazis, racists' and said they should be shot. Paulin had earlier compared Israelis to Nazis in a poem referring to Israeli soldiers as the 'Zionist SS'.[74] In the demonstrations against British military action against Iraq in 2003, protesters routinely carried placards juxtaposing the star of David with the swastika. These demonstrations, under the slogan 'Stop the invasion of Iraq – Free Palestine', were organised by the Stop the War Coalition, which is built around Socialist Workers Party activists.

A significant recent innovation of anti-Zionism on the left is the belief that although the mass murder of the Jews by the Nazis occurred, it was only one genocide amongst many in the last century and deserves no privileged attention such as Holocaust memorial days. On the contrary, Norman Finkelstein, the American Jewish leftist largely responsible for propagating and popularising this line, maintains that 'the Holocaust' is a cultural construct fabricated by Jews to inculcate guilt in Western nations, extract reparations money for Israel, and suppress criticism of Zionism.[75]

Since the 1990s, the notion that rich Jews comprise a worldwide network of power and influence that is covertly behind world affairs has migrated from the right to the left. In part this reflects the political realignment of Jews in the USA and the emergence of Jews in the ranks of the neo-conservatives. The association of American Jews with the right has become a routine stereotype in much the same way that Russian Jews were once tarred with Bolshevism. This stereotyping persists, despite the fact that in the 1980s and 1990s American Jews such as Amitai Etzioni were credited with pioneering communitarian policies that had a great influence on the US Democrats and the mainstream left, especially in the UK. The stereotyping of Jews in this way owes much to anti-American and anti-globalisation campaigners who routinely conflate the stated goals of 'Jewish neo-conservatives' in Washington with Israeli policy. The fallacy of this position lies in a set of dubious assumptions: that all neo-conservatives are Jews, which they are not; that a person who is Jewish must have Jewish allegiances, which is not so; and the a priori assumption that if neo-conservative geopolitical aspirations coincide with Israeli interests, they owe their inspiration to the fulfilment of Jewish rather than US national goals. Anti-American and anti-globalisation polemicists who depict US policy in Iraq as serving Israel's interests, or Israeli repression of the Palestinians as sanctioned by a Jewish-dominated Washington, are transforming and rehabilitating the myth of a worldwide Jewish network operating with selfish and malign intentions.[76]

The recent ethnic politics of the far left, and what the mainstream left sees as the importance of recognising the demands of Muslim voters in countries with large Muslim populations, has added to the volatility of this ideological brew. The Muslim communities are variegated and diverse, so it is dangerous to generalise, but many Muslims feel that the relatively benign history of Jewish–Muslim relations renders them immune to charges of anti-semitism. Muslims rightly feel no responsibility for Nazi atrocities against the Jews and, on the contrary, feel aggrieved that with the creation of Israel in 1948 Palestinian Arabs paid the price for Christian aggression against the Jews of Europe. Many young Muslims in Britain and France regard Jews as part of a wealthy, powerful white establishment that excludes them, and cannot conceive that Jews were once the victims of institutional racism. This renders politically engaged Muslims insensitive to Jewish anxieties and vulnerabilities, and places a heavy responsibility on the entire Left when it addresses their concerns. For, as the recent report of the European Monitoring Centre on Racism and Xenophobia demonstrated, there is a correlation between anti-Jewish violence and rhetoric and events in the Middle East. The report showed that Arab-speaking Muslims are accessing crude anti-semitic propaganda from Arab satellite TV stations, while most members of the Muslim communities have access to internet sites purveying similar material from Islamist or right-wing groups. In these circumstances, the Left in all its varieties needs to reflect on the way it presents the Israel/Palestine conflict and debates the place and the role of Jews in the world.[77]

11 Conclusions

This essay has attempted to show how the relationship between Jews and the Left has evolved and changed in a mutual dynamic over 150 years. Jewish values and the Jewish historical experience created a certain affinity for socialism amongst Jews, but there was never an intrinsic symbiosis (as right-wing anti-semites alleged), and social change, particularly upward social mobility, derogated from Jewish enthusiasm for the Left. During the nineteenth century, Jews welcomed the emancipatory thrust of socialism, but the Left was never unconditional about what it offered to Jews. In a sense, both had misconceptions about what civic equality was supposed to deliver. Jews aspired to both equality and the preservation of a vestigial Jewish identity; the Left could not appreciate the Jewish desire for continuity and interpreted this as 'clannishness' or apartness. Jews wanted to pursue whatever economic opportunities came their way; the Left saw this as rampant individualism.

The creation of large, urban proletarian Jewish communities obliged the Left to reconsider its slighting view of Jews as *homo economicus,* personified by the figure of Rothschild. Although some purblind observers persisted in seeing Jewish workers as merely entrepreneurs in the making, others perceived them as a significant addition to the workers' front. Between 1880 and 1950, Jewish trades unions flourished in London, Paris, New York, Buenos Aires and Johannesburg. A vibrant secular Jewish socialist culture complemented the labour movement as a whole and Jews graduated to the upper reaches of leadership in every single socialist organisation.

However, there was still a mismatch between the expectations of the Left and Jewish aspirations. Socialists continued to see separate Jewish labour organisations as a device to acculturate, integrate and ultimately assimilate the Jews. With a few exceptions, the Left utterly rejected Jewish nationalism in the form of demands for national-cultural autonomy in the diaspora or Zionism. Socialists and Jews were united in their resistance to fascism and Nazism as long as this was premised on the defence of individual human and civil rights. The 'pink generation' of the 1930s gave the impression of a virtual synthesis between socialism and Jews, but anti-fascism masked persistent fractures along the lines of class and ethnicity.

The unease of the Left became more apparent in the post-war years when 'Jewish difference' took on a national form. While unequivocally upholding the rights of Diaspora Jews, the Left was ambivalent towards Israel. As long as Israel appeared to embody left-wing aspiration, this ambivalence was latent. Once Israel departed from its socialist trajectory and in effect demanded acceptance for what it was, and not what the Left hoped it might become, the trouble started. While the mainstream old left grudgingly accommodated itself to Israel's existence, the far left and New Left saw no redeeming features in Israel.

Anti-Zionist discourse on the Left has ranged from claims

that Zionists conspired with Nazis in the destruction of the Jews so as to guilt-trip the world into accepting a Jewish state, to the doctrinaire rejection of Jewish collective rights. However, when seen in the *longue durée*, there is nothing intrinsically 'new' about elements of the Left depicting Jews in negative stereotypes as rich, powerful, conspiratorial or the agents of international finance. While much of the rhetoric employed since 2000 has been directly related to the Israel/Palestine conflict, it draws on tropes that are embedded in socialist ideologies stretching back to pre-Marxist socialism. Criticism of Israeli government policy in relation to the Palestinians, and on other issues, is totally legitimate, but some parts of the Left have not broken free of the nineteenth-century Marxist dogma that the Jews are merely a religious group and not a people that has a right to national self-determination in its own land.

In the last few years, the Left has adopted the Palestinian cause even more fervently, partly due to the deepening crisis in the Middle East and the appalling suffering of the Palestinian Arabs, and partly out of eagerness to engage communities in the Muslim diaspora. Its ingrained anti-Americanism has found a ready echo here thanks to what many Muslims see as the anti-Islamic aspects of the US 'war against terrorism'. The danger of this development is that anti-Jewish currents circulating in parts of the Muslim world are melding with the ambivalent attitudes of the Left towards the Jews to form a noxious concoction. The Left has not always taken anti-semitism seriously, and there are signs that in treating Jewish fears about anti-Jewish sentiment as merely a device to muzzle criticism of Israel – what Paul

Foot has called 'bleating about anti-semitism' (*Guardian*, 5 March 2002) – it is in danger of repeating the historic error of those like Bebel who dismissed hatred of Jews and threats to their well-being as merely a delusion and the symptom of an ephemeral conflict.

In the light of contemporary trends it may suit Jewish conservatives to gloss over the distinguished and distinctive role of Jews in the Left throughout its history and to dismiss Jewish socialists as deluded, even 'self-hating'. But as this essay has tried to show, it is impossible to deny the closeness and the achievements of this relationship. The great Jewish proletarian communities have long gone, and the secular–socialist Yiddish civilisation of Eastern Europe has been destroyed by the Nazis or dismantled by the Soviets, but their legacy continues. It is evident in the battered but resilient Israeli left, and the doggedly left-of-centre politics and sentiments of a majority of Jews throughout the Jewish world. The great emancipatory project to achieve civic equality and social justice brought Jews and the Left together in the aftermath of the French Revolution and, despite all the ambivalences of their relationship, this noble cause remains capable of uniting them today.

Notes

1 Introduction

1 The classic study in this genre is Edmund Silberner, *Sozialisten zur Judenfrage* (1962). Silberner published numerous influential articles on the subject in English in the 1950s and 1960s. Leonard Schapiro, 'The role of Jews in the Russian revolutionary movement', *Slavonic and East European Review* 40 (1961–62), 148–67 [repr. Ezra Mendelsohn ed., *Essential Papers on Jews and the Left* (1997)], 300–21. See also Robert Wistrich, *Revolutionary Jews from Marx to Trotsky* (1976) and *Socialism and the Jews. The Dilemmas of Assimilation in Germany and Austria-Hungary* (1982).

2 See Ezra Mendelsohn ed., *Essential Papers on Jews and the Left* (1997), hereafter EP.

3 For a comprehensive survey see George Lichtheim, *A Short History of Socialism* (1970) and Donald Sassoon, *One Hundred Years of Socialism: The West European Left in the Twentieth Century* (1996).

4 Michael Walzer, 'Liberalism and the Jews: historical affinities, contemporary necessities', in Peter Medding ed., *Studies in Contemporary Jewry* vol. 11, *Jews and Politics in a Changing World* (1995), 3–10. Cf. James Campbell, 'Beyond the Pale: Jewish immigration and the South

African Left' in Milton Shain and Richard Mendelsohn eds, *Memories, Realities and Dreams: Aspects of the South African Jewish Experience* (2000), 96–162.

2 Enlightenment and revolution: the sources of inspiration and ambivalence

5 For overviews see Lloyd P. Gartner, *History of the Jews in Modern Time* (2001) and David Vital, *A People Apart. The Jews in Europe 1789–1939* (1999). On court and port Jews, see David Cesarani ed., *Port Jews: Jewish communities in cosmopolitan maritime trading centres 1650–1950* (2002).

6 Arthur Hertzberg, *The French Enlightenment and the Jews* (1968).

7 Adam Sutcliffe, *Judaism and Enlightenment* (2003), 228–243. See also Enzo Traverso, *The Marxists and the Jewish Question: The History of a Debate 1843-1943* (1994), 2–4.

8 The best analysis is in Hertzberg, *The French Enlightenment and the Jews.*

9 Ritchie Robertson ed., *The German–Jewish Dialogue: An Anthology of Literary Texts 1749–1993* (1999), 9, and *The 'Jewish Question' in German Literature 1749–1939. Emancipation and its Discontents* (1999), 32–45.

10 David Sorkin, *Moses Mendelssohn and the Religious Enlightenment* (1996).

11 Robertson, *The 'Jewish Question' in German Literature 1749–1939*, 45–50.

12 Paula Hyman, *The Jews of Modern France* (1998), 17–35.

13 Hyman, *The Jews of Modern France*, 17–35.

14 Vital, *A People Apart*, 212–25. Amos Elon, *The Pity of It*

All: A Portrait of Jews in Germany 1743–1933 (2002), 133.

15 For a joint portrait of Börne and Heine see Elon, *The Pity of It All*, 101–48.

3 Socialism and the Jews from Saint Simon to Karl Marx

16 Jacob Katz, *From Prejudice to Destruction* (1980), 120–22. Vital, *A People Apart*, 200–202.

17 Katz, *From Prejudice to Destruction*, 124–8; Vital, *A People Apart*, 202–5. George Lichtheim, 'Socialism and the Jews', *Dissent* (July–August 1968), 316.

18 There is a large literature on Marx and the Jews. For a pithy discussion, see Wistrich, *Revolutionary Jews*, 27–45. For extended treatments, see Isaiah Berlin, *Karl Marx* (1963) and Julius Carlbach, *Karl Marx and the Radical Critique of Judaism* (1978).

19 Katz, *From Prejudice to Destruction*, 164–70; Vital, *A People Apart*, 190–4.

20 Traverso, *The Marxists and the Jewish Question*, 17–22; Wistrich, *Revolutionary Jews*, 27–45 and *Socialism and the Jews*, 25–9.

21 Moses Hess, *Rome and Jerusalem*, trans. Meyer Waxman [(1862) 1918], 43, 48–9, 58–9, 115–17, 145–66. Isaiah Berlin, 'The life and opinions of Moses Hess', EP, 21–57; Shlomo Aveniri, *The Making of Modern Zionism* (1981), 40–46.

4 Social democracy and the Jews

22 Wistrich, *Revolutionary Jews*, 47–58.

23 Wistrich, *Socialism and the Jews*, 72–89, 90–125. See also Traverso, *The Marxists and the Jewish Question*, 25–7.

24 Eric Cham, *The Dreyfus Affair in French Politics and*

Society (1994), 96–8. On Lazare, see Nelly Wilson, *Bernard Lazare: Antisemitism and the Problem of Jewish Identity in Nineteenth Century France* (1978).

25 Wistrich, *Socialism and the Jews*, 133–4; Jack Jacobs, *On Socialists and the 'Jewish Question' After Marx* (1992), 19; Traverso, *The Marxists and the Jewish Question*, 63–4, 82–7.

26 Traverso, *The Marxists and the Jewish Question*, 60–61. See also, Wistrich, *Revolutionary Jews*, 98–114.

27 Traverso, *The Marxists and the Jewish Question*, 66–7. See also Wistrich, *Revolutionary Jews*, 115–24 and Wistrich, *Socialism and the Jews*, 175–261, 299–348.

28 Jacobs, *On Socialists and the 'Jewish Question' After Marx*, 44–62.

29 Wistrich, *Revolutionary Jews*, 76–92. Cf Jacobs, *On Socialists and the 'Jewish Question' After Marx*, 76–84.

5 Jews, socialism, and revolution in Eastern Europe

30 For the background, see Nora Levin, *Jewish Socialist Movements 1871–1917* (1978), 3–20, and Eric Haberer, *Jews and Revolution in Nineteenth-century Russia* (1995), 17–69.

31 Haberer, *Jews and Revolution in Nineteenth-century Russia*, 68–9, 74–84. Cf. Traverso, *The Marxists and the Jewish Question*, 39–51.

32 Haberer, *Jews and Revolution in Nineteenth-century Russia*, 94–200.

33 Haberer, *Jews and Revolution in Nineteenth-century Russia*, 204–5; I. M. Aronson, *Troubled Waters. The Origins of the 1881 Anti-Jewish Pogroms in Russia* (1990).

34 Jonathan Frankel, *Prophecy and Politics: Socialism, Nationalism and the Russian Jews, 1862–1917* (1981), 97–107.

35 Frankel, *Prophecy and Politics*, 173–5 and 'The roots of "Jewish Socialism" (1881–1892): from "Populism" to "Cosmopolitanism"?', EP, 58–77; Israel Getzler, 'A grandson of the Haskalah', EP, 275–99, a summary of his *Martov: a Political Biography of a Russian Social Democrat* (1967).

36 Ezra Mendelsohn, *Class Struggle in the Pale: The Formative Years of the Jewish Workers' Movement in Tsarist Russia* (1970); Henry Tobias, *The Jewish Bund in Russia – from its origins to 1905* (1972).

37 Tobias, *The Jewish Bund in Russia – from its origins to 1905*.

6 Socialists and the Jewish labour movement

38 John Klier and Shlomo Lambroza eds, *Pogroms: Anti-Jewish Violence in Modern Russian History* (1992).

39 Nancy Green ed., *Jewish Workers in the Modern Diaspora* (1998).

40 Lloyd P. Gartner, *The Jewish Immigrant in England, 1870–1914* (1973 edn).

41 John Garrard, *The English and Immigration* (1971); Bernard Gainer, *The Alien Invasion: The Origins of the Aliens Act* (1972); David Feldman, 'The Importance of Being English. Jewish immigration and the decay of liberal England' in D. Feldman and Gareth Stedman Jones eds, *Metropolis London: Histories and Representations since 1800* (1989), 56–84.

42 William Fishman, *East End Jewish Radicals, 1875–1914* (1975); David Feldman, *Englishmen and Jews: Social Relations and Political Culture, 1840–1914* (1992), pt. 3; A. J. Kershen, *Uniting the Tailors: Trades Unionism amongst the Tailors of London and Leeds, 1870–1939* (1995).

43 David Englander, 'Booth's Jews: the presentation of Jews and Judaism in *Life and Labour of the London Poor*', *Victorian Studies* 32:4 (1989), 551–72.

44 Colin Holmes, *Anti-Semitism and British Society, 1876–1939* (1979), 81–8, 107–15.

45 Frankel, *Prophecy and Politics*, 453–509; Arthur Goren, 'Socialist politics on the Lower East Side' in his *The Politics and Public Culture of American Jews* (1999), 83–99. And see Gerald Sorin, *The Prophetic Minority: American Jewish Immigrant Radicals 1880–1920* (1985).

7 Zionism and the Left

46 David Vital, *The Origins of Zionism* (1975); Walter Laqueur, *A History of Zionism* (1972), 84–135.

47 Shlomo Avineri, *The Making of Modern Zionism: The Intellectual Origins of the Jewish State* (1981), 125–39.

48 Avineri, *The Making of Modern Zionism*, 140–50. Cf. Traverso, *The Marxists and the Jewish Question*, 110–22.

49 Wistrich, *Socialism and the Jews*, 141–72.

8 Jews and the Left in the face of Fascism and Nazism

50 Mark Levene, *War, Jews and the New Europe* (1992); David Vital, *Zionism: The Crucial Phase* (1987).

51 Gizela Lebzelter, *Political Anti-semitism in England 1918–1939* (1978), 12–29; Colin Holmes, *Anti-semitism in*

British Society (1979), 144–60; Sharman Kadish, *Bolsheviks and British Jews* (1992).

52 David Cesarani, 'An embattled minority: the Jews in Britain during World War One' in T. Kushner and K. Lunn eds, *The Politics of Marginality* (1990), 61–81, 'Anti-Zionist politics and political anti-semitism in England, 1920–1924', *Patterns of Prejudice*, 23:1 (1989), 28–45, 'Anti-alienism in England after the First World War,' *Immigrants and Minorities*, 6:1 (March 1987), 5–29, and 'The anti-Jewish career of Sir William Joynson-Hicks, cabinet minister', *Journal of Contemporary History*, 24:4 (1989), 61–82.

53 On the anti-Jewish animus behind the Palmer Raids, see Zosa Szajkowski, *Jews, Wars, and Communism*, vol. 2, *The Impact of the 1919–1920 Red Scare on American Jewish Life* (1974), John Higham, *Strangers in the Land* (1955) and Leonard Dinnerstein, *Anti-Semitism in America* (1994). Benjamin Pinkus, *The Jews of the Soviet Union: The History of a Minority* (1988); Zvi Gitelman, *Jewish Nationality and Soviet Politics: The Jewish Sections of the CPSU, 1917–1930* (1972); Allan Kagedan, *Soviet Zion: The Quest for a Russian Jewish Homeland* (1994).

54 Richard Crossman ed., *The God That Failed* (1950) is almost a collective biography of Jews of the Left in this period; Arno Lustig, *Salud die Helden* (1992).

55 Tony Kushner and Nadia Valman eds, *Remembering Cable Street* (1999); Henry Srebrnik, *London Jews and British Communism, 1935–1945* (1995); Phil Piratin, *Our Flag Stays Red* (1975 edn).

56 Joseph Gorny, *The British Labour Movement and Zionism*

1917–1948 (1983), 3-47; David Cesarani, 'Anti-Zionist politics and political anti-semitism in England, 1920–1924', *Patterns of Prejudice*, 23:1 (1989), 28–45.

57 Gorny, *The British Labour Movement and Zionism*, 91–5 and Geoffrey Alderman, *The Jewish Community in British Politics* (1983), 111–15. Deborah Osmond, 'British Jewry and Labour politics 1918–1939', in Christine Collette and Stephen Bird eds, *Jews, Labour and the Left, 1918–48* (2000), 55–70 and Christine Collette, 'The utopian visions of Labour Zionism, British Labour and the Labour and Socialist International in the 1930s', ibid., 71–92.

58 Jacobs, *On Socialists and the 'Jewish Question' after Marx*, 61–3; Collette, 'The utopian visions of Labour Zionism, British Labour and the Labour and Socialist International in the 1930s'; Joseph Nedava, *Trotsky and the Jews* (1972), 202–12; Kenneth Slepyan, 'The Soviet partisan movement and the Holocaust', *Holocaust and Genocide Studies*, 14:1 (2000) 1–27; Renée Poznanski, 'Reflections on Jewish resistance and Jewish resistants in France', *Jewish Social Studies*, 1:3 (1995) 68–82; Isabelle Tombs, 'Szmul Zygielbojm, the British Labour Party and the Holocaust' in Collette and Bird eds, *Jews, Labour and the Left, 1918–48*, 122–40.

59 Gorny, *The British Labour Movement and Zionism*, 178–83.

9 The Left and the Jews from post-war to Cold War

60 Bernard Wasserstein, *Vanishing Diaspora: The Jews in Europe Since 1945* (1996) provides the best overview.

W. D. Rubinstein, *The Left, the Right and the Jews* (1982), 77–117.

61 Wasserstein, *Vanishing Diaspora*, 36–57. For detailed accounts see Lewis Rapoport, *Stalin's War Against the Jews* (1990) and Arkady Vaksberg, *Stalin Against the Jews* (1994).

62 Peter Brod, 'Soviet–Israeli relations 1948–56' in Robert Wistrich ed., *The Left Against Zion* (1979) [LAZ], 50–70.

63 On Europe, see Wasserstein, *Vanishing Diaspora*, 62–82. For the USA, Edward S. Shapiro, *A Time for Healing: American Jewry since World War II* (1992), 34–38, 94–122. Richard Crossman MP is a prime example of a parliamentarian enraptured by Israel.

64 François Bondy, 'Communist attitudes in France and Italy to the Six Day War', LAZ, 166–86.

65 Stanley Rothman and S. Robert Lichter, *Roots of Radicalism: Jews, Christians, and the New Left* (1982), 21–5, 31–3, 81–3; Arnold Foster, 'American radicals and Israel', LAZ, 220–25.

66 Earl Raab, 'American Blacks and Israel' in Robert Wistrich ed., *Antizionism and Antisemitism in the Contemporary World* (1990) [AACW], 155–70. See Hasia Diner, *In the Almost Promised Land: American Jews and Blacks, 1915–1935* (1995) for a balanced appraisal.

67 W. D. Rubinstein, *The Left, the Right and the Jews* (1982), 77–117. The drift to the right in England is documented in Geoffrey Alderman, *The Jewish Community in British Politics* and *London Jewry and London Politics 1889–1986* (1989). See also Arthur Liebman, 'The ties that bind: Jewish support for the Left in America', EP, 342–54.

68 Alderman, *London Jewry and London Politics*, 121, 127–38.
69 Steve Cohen, *That's Funny, You Don't Look Anti-semitic* (1984) for an analysis of left anti-semitism of the period.
70 David Cesarani, 'The Perdition Affair', AACW, 53–60.
71 Campbell, 'Beyond the Pale', 156. Glenn Frankel, *Rivonia's Children* (1999) tells the story of Jews and the ANC struggle.

10 The Left and the Jews since the end of the Cold War

72 Peter Pulzer, 'The new antisemitism, or when is a taboo not a taboo?', Paul Iganski and Barry Kosmin eds, *A New Antisemitism?* (2003), 79–101 and in the same volume, Ronnie Fraser, 'Understanding trades union hostility towards Israel and its consequences for Anglo-Jewry', 258–66. Melanie Phillips, *Observer*, 22 February 2004. European Monitoring Centre on Racism and Xenophobia, *Report on Manifestations of anti-Semitism in the European Union*, November 2003, 8.
73 Interview with Colin Brown and Chris Hastings in *Sunday Telegraph*, 4 May 2003.
74 Rod Liddell, *Guardian*, G2, 17 April 2002.
75 Norman Finkelstein, *The Holocaust Industry: Reflections on the Exploitation of Jewish Suffering* (2000).
76 Naomi Klein, *Guardian*, 25 April 2002. For a deeper analysis, see Alvin H. Rosenfeld, *Anti-Americanism and Anti-semitism: A New Frontier of Bigotry* (2003).
77 See European Monitoring Centre on Racism and Xenophobia, *Report on Manifestations of anti-Semitism in the European Union*, 32–39.

Bibliography

Geoffrey Alderman, *The Jewish Community in British Politics* (1983)

Geoffrey Alderman, *London Jewry and London Politics 1889–1986* (1989)

I. M. Aronson, *Troubled Waters. The Origins of the 1881 Anti-Jewish Pogroms in Russia* (1990)

Shlomo Avineri, *The Making of Modern Zionism: The Intellectual Origins of the Jewish State* (1981)

Isaiah Berlin, *Karl Marx* (1963)

Isaiah Berlin, 'The life and opinions of Moses Hess', in Mendelsohn ed., *Essential Papers on Jews and the Left*, 21–57

François Bondy, 'Communist attitudes in France and Italy to the Six Day War', in Wistrich ed., *The Left Against Zion*, 166–86

Peter Brod, 'Soviet–Israeli relations 1948–56' in Wistrich ed., *The Left Against Zion* (1979), 50–70

James Campbell, 'Beyond the Pale: Jewish immigration and the South African Left' in Shain and Mendelsohn eds, *Memories, Realities and Dreams: Aspects of the South African Jewish Experience* (2000), 96–162

Julius Carlbach, *Karl Marx and the Radical Critique of Judaism* (1978)

David Cesarani ed., *Port Jews: Jewish Communities in Cosmopolitan Maritime Trading Centres 1650–1950* (2002)

David Cesarani, 'An embattled minority: the Jews in Britain during World War One' in Kushner and Lunn eds, *The Politics of Marginality*, (1990), 61–81

David Cesarani, 'Anti-Zionist politics and political anti-semitism in England, 1920–1924', *Patterns of Prejudice*, 23:1 (1989), 28–45

David Cesarani, 'Anti-alienism in England after the First World War,' *Immigrants and Minorities*, 6:1 (March 1987), 5–29

David Cesarani, 'The anti-Jewish career of Sir William Joynson-Hicks, cabinet minister', *Journal of Contemporary History*, 24:4 (1989), 61–82

David Cesarani, 'The Perdition Affair', in Wistrich ed., *Antizionism and Antisemitism*, 53–60

Eric Cham, *The Dreyfus Affair in French Politics and Society* (1994)

Steve Cohen, *That's Funny, You Don't Look Anti-semitic* (1984)

Christine Collette and Stephen Bird eds, *Jews, Labour and the Left, 1918–48* (2000)

Christine Collette, 'The utopian visions of Labour Zionism, British Labour and the Labour and Socialist International in the 1930s', in Collette and Bird eds, *Jews, Labour and the Left, 1918–48*, 71–92.

Richard Crossman MP, *A Nation Reborn: The Israel of Weizmann, Bevin and Ben-Gurion* (1960)

Richard Crossman MP ed., *The God That Failed* (1950)

Hasia Diner, *In the Almost Promised Land. American Jews and Blacks, 1915–1935* (1995)

Leonard Dinnerstein, *Anti-semitism in America* (1994)

Amos Elon, *The Pity of It All: A Portrait of Jews in Germany 1743–1933* (2002)

David Englander, 'Booth's Jews: the presentation of Jews and Judaism in *Life and Labour of the London Poor*', *Victorian Studies* 32:4 (1989), 551–72

European Monitoring Centre on Racism and Xenophobia, *Report on Manifestations of Anti-semitism in the European Union*, November 2003

David Feldman, 'The importance of being English. Jewish immigration and the decay of liberal England' in Feldman and Stedman Jones eds., *Metropolis London: Histories and Representations Since 1800* (1989), 56–84

David Feldman, *Englishmen and Jews: Social Relations and Political Culture, 1840–1914* (1992)

David Feldman and Gareth Stedman Jones eds., *Metropolis London: Histories and Representations Since 1800* (1989)

Norman Finkelstein, *The Holocaust Industry: Reflections on the Exploitation of Jewish Suffering* (2000)

William Fishman, *East End Jewish Radicals, 1875–1914* (1975)

Arnold Foster, 'American radicals and Israel', in Wistrich ed., *The Left Against Zion*, 220–25

Glenn Frankel, *Rivonia's Children* (1999)

Jonathan Frankel, 'The roots of "Jewish Socialism" (1881–1892): from "Populism" to "Cosmopolitanism"?', in Mendelsohn ed., *Essential Papers on Jews and the Left*, 58–77

Jonathan Frankel, *Prophecy and Politics: Socialism, Nationalism and the Russian Jews, 1862–1917* (1981)
Ronnie Fraser, 'Understanding trades union hostility towards Israel and its consequences for Anglo-Jewry', in Iganski and Kosmin eds, *A New Antisemitism?*, 258–66
Bernard Gainer, *The Alien Invasion - The Origins of the Aliens Act* (1972)
John Garrard, *The English and Immigration* (1971)
Lloyd P. Gartner, *The Jewish Immigrant in England, 1870–1914* (1973 edn)
Lloyd P. Gartner, *History of the Jews in Modern Time* (2001)
Israel Getzler, 'A grandson of the Haskalah', in Mendelsohn ed., *Essential Papers on Jews and the Left*, 275–99
Israel Getzler, *Martov: A Political Biography of a Russian Social Democrat* (1967)
Zvi Gitelman, *Jewish Nationality and Soviet Politics: The Jewish Sections of the CPSU, 1917–1930* (1972)
Arthur Goren, 'Socialist politics on the Lower East Side' in his *The Politics and Public Culture of American Jews* (1999), 83–99
Joseph Gorny, *The British Labour Movement and Zionism 1917–1948* (1983)
Nancy Green ed., *Jewish Workers in the Modern Diaspora* (1998)
Eric Haberer, *Jews and Revolution in Nineteenth-century Russia* (1995)
Arthur Hertzberg, *The French Enlightenment and the Jews* (1968)
Moses Hess, *Rome and Jerusalem*, trans. Meyer Waxman ([1862] 1918)

John Higham, *Strangers in the Land* (1955)
Colin Holmes, *Anti-semitism and British Society, 1876–1939* (1979)
Paula Hyman, *The Jews of Modern France* (1998)
Paul Iganski and Barry Kosmin eds, *A New Antisemitism?* (2003)
Jack Jacobs, *On Socialists and the 'Jewish Question' After Marx* (1992)
Bernard Johnpoll, *The Politics of Futility: The General Jewish Workers Bund of Poland, 1917–1934* (1967)
Sharman Kadish, *Bolsheviks and British Jews* (1992)
Allan Kagedan, *Soviet Zion: The Quest for a Russian Jewish Homeland* (1994)
Jacob Katz, *From Prejudice to Destruction* (1980)
Anne Kershen, *Uniting the Tailors: Trades Unionism amongst the Tailors of London and Leeds, 1870–1939* (1995)
John Klier and Shlomo Lambroza eds, *Pogroms: Anti-Jewish Violence in Modern Russian History* (1992)
Tony Kushner and Ken Lunn eds, *The Politics of Marginality* (1990)
Tony Kushner and Nadia Valman eds, *Remembering Cable Street* (1999)
Walter Laqueur, *A History of Zionism* (1972)
Gizela Lebzelter, *Political Anti-semitism in England 1918–1939* (1978)
Mark Levene, *War, Jews and the New Europe* (1992)
Nora Levin, *Jewish Socialist Movements 1871–1917* (1978)
George Lichtheim, 'Socialism and the Jews', *Dissent* (July–August 1968)
George Lichtheim, *A Short History of Socialism* (1970)

Arthur Liebman, 'The ties that bind: Jewish support for the Left in America', in Mendelsohn ed., *Essential Papers on Jews and the Left*, 342–54

Arthur Liebman, *Jews and the Left* (1979)

Arno Lustig, *Salud die Helden* (1992)

Peter Medding ed., *Studies in Contemporary Jewry*, vol. 11, *Jews and Politics in a Changing World* (1995)

Ezra Mendelsohn, *Class Struggle in the Pale: The Formative Years of the Jewish Workers' Movement in Tsarist Russia* (1970)

Ezra Mendelsohn ed., *Essential Papers on Jews and the Left* (1997)

Joseph Nedava, *Trotsky and the Jews* (1972)

Deborah Osmond, 'British Jewry and Labour politics 1918–1939', in Collette and Bird eds, *Jews, Labour and the Left, 1918–48*, 55–70

Benjamin Pinkus, *The Jews of the Soviet Union: The History of a Minority* (1988)

Phil Piratin, *Our Flag Stays Red* (1975 edn)

Anthony Polonsky ed., *Polin*, vol. 9, *Jews, Poles, Socialism: The Failure of an Ideal* (1996)

Renée Poznanski, 'Reflections on Jewish resistance and Jewish resistants in France', *Jewish Social Studies*, 1:3 (1995) 68–82

Peter Pulzer, 'The new anti-semitism, or when is a taboo not a taboo?' in Iganski and Kosmin eds, *A New Antisemitism?* (2003) 79–101

Earl Raab, 'American Blacks and Israel' in Wistrich ed., *Antizionism and Antisemitism in the Contemporary World* (1990), 155–70

Lewis Rapoport, *Stalin's War Against the Jews* (1990)
Ritchie Robertson ed., *The German–Jewish Dialogue. An Anthology of Literary Texts 1749–1993* (1999)
Ritchie Robertson ed., *The 'Jewish Question' in German Literature 1749–1939: Emancipation and its Discontents* (1999)
Alvin H. Rosenfeld, *Anti-Americanism and Anti-semitism: A New Frontier of Bigotry* (2003)
Stanley Rothman and S. Robert Lichter, *Roots of Radicalism: Jews, Christians, and the New Left* (1982)
W. D. Rubinstein, *The Left, the Right and the Jews* (1982)
Donald Sassoon, *One Hundred Years of Socialism: The West European Left in the Twentieth Century* (1996)
Leonard Schapiro, 'The role of Jews in the Russian revolutionary movement', *Slavonic and East European Review* 40 (1961–62) 148–67
Jeff Schatz, *The Generation: The Rise and Fall of the Jewish Communists in Poland* (1991)
Anita Shapira, *Berl: The Biography of a Socialist Zionist, Berl Katznelson 1887–1944* (1984)
Edward S. Shapiro, *A Time for Healing: American Jewry since World War II* (1992)
Edmund Silberner, *Sozialisten zur Judenfrage* (1962)
Kenneth Slepyan, 'The Soviet partisan movement and the Holocaust', *Holocaust and Genocide Studies*, 14:1 (2000) 1–27
Gerald Sorin, *The Prophetic Minority: American Jewish Immigrant Radicals 1880–1920* (1985)
David Sorkin, *Moses Mendelssohn and the Religious Enlightenment* (1996)

Henry Srebrnik, *London Jews and British Communism, 1935–1945* (1995)
Adam Sutcliffe, *Judaism and Enlightenment* (2003)
Zosa Szajkowski, *Jews, Wars, and Communism*, 2 vols (1974)
Shabetai Teveth, *Ben Gurion: The Burning Ground, 1886–1940* (1987)
Henry Tobias, *The Jewish Bund in Russia – From its Origins to 1905* (1972)
Isabelle Tombs, 'Szmul Zygielbojm, the British Labour Party and the Holocaust' in Collette and Bird eds, *Jews, Labour and the Left, 1918–48*. 122–40.
Enzo Traverso, *The Marxists and the Jewish Question. The History of a Debate 1843–1943* (1994)
Arkady Vaksberg, *Stalin Against the Jews* (1994)
David Vital, *The Origins of Zionism* (1975)
David Vital, *Zionism: The Crucial Phase* (1987)
David Vital, *A People Apart: The Jews in Europe 1789–1939* (1999)
Michael Walzer, 'Liberalism and the Jews: historical affinities, contemporary necessities', in Medding ed., *Studies in Contemporary Jewry* vol. 11, *Jews and Politics in a Changing World* (1995), 3–10
Bernard Wasserstein, *Vanishing Diaspora: The Jews in Europe Since 1945* (1996)
Geoffrey Wigoder ed., *Dictionary of Jewish Biography* (1991)
Nelly Wilson, *Bernard Lazare: Antisemitism and the Problem of Jewish Identity in Nineteenth Century France* (1978)
Robert Wistrich, *Revolutionary Jews from Marx to Trotsky* (1976)

Robert Wistrich, *Socialism and the Jews: The Dilemmas of Assimilation in Germany and Austria-Hungary* (1982).
Robert Wistrich ed., *The Left Against Zion* (1979)
Robert Wistrich ed., *Antizionism and Antisemitism in the Contemporary World* (1990)

www.ingramcontent.com/pod-product-compliance
Ingram Content Group UK Ltd.
Pitfield, Milton Keynes, MK11 3LW, UK
UKHW042002190726
13854UKWH00005B/2131